Turning the Page on
Complex TEXTS

**Differentiated Scaffolds for
Close Reading Instruction**

DIANE LAPP, BARBARA MOSS,
MARIA C. GRANT, & KELLY JOHNSON

Solution Tree | Press

a division of
Solution Tree

555 North Morton Street
Bloomington, IN 47404
800.733.6786 (toll free) / 812.336.7700
FAX: 812.336.7790

email: info@SolutionTree.com
SolutionTree.com

Visit **go.SolutionTree.com/literacy** to download the reproducibles in this book.

Printed in the United States of America

20 19 18 17 16   1 2 3 4 5

Library of Congress Cataloging-in-Publication Data

Names: Lapp, Diane, author.
Title: Turning the page on complex texts : differentiated scaffolds for close
   reading instruction / Diane Lapp, Barbara Moss, Maria C. Grant, and Kelly
   Johnson.
Description: Bloomington, IN : Solution Tree Press, [2016] | Includes
   bibliographical references and index.
Identifiers: LCCN 2016009093 | ISBN 9781935249467 (perfect bound)
Subjects: LCSH: Reading (Elementary) | Reading (Secondary) | Individualized
   reading instruction. | Group work in education.
Classification: LCC LB1573 .L294 2016 | DDC 372.4--dc23 LC record available at https://lccn.loc.
gov/2016009093

Solution Tree
Jeffrey C. Jones, CEO
Edmund M. Ackerman, President

Solution Tree Press
President: Douglas M. Rife
Editorial Director: Tonya Maddox Cupp
Managing Production Editor: Caroline Weiss
Senior Production Editor: Tara Perkins
Senior Editor: Amy Rubenstein
Copy Editor: Ashante K. Thomas
Proofreader: Elisabeth Abrams
Text and Cover Designer: Laura Kagemann

Acknowledgments

The authors wish to thank all of the teachers who have welcomed us into their classrooms. We learn so much from being your partners, and we hope this text addresses the many questions you're asking about scaffolding instruction during and after a close reading.

Solution Tree Press would like to thank the following reviewers:

Dana Johansen
English Teacher
Greenwich Academy
Greenwich, Connecticut

Cathy Mere
Literacy Specialist
Darby Creek Elementary School
Hilliard, Ohio

Nancy Witherell
Professor of Reading
Bridgewater State University
Bridgewater, Massachusetts

Visit **go.SolutionTree.com/literacy**
to download the reproducibles in this book.

Table of Contents

About the Authors

Diane Lapp, EdD, is a distinguished professor of education at San Diego State University and an English teacher and literacy coach at Health Sciences High and Middle College (HSHMC) in San Diego, California. Previously, she taught elementary and middle school grade levels. Diane focuses on instruction that supports learning for a diverse range of students. Her career is founded on the idea that motivation and well-planned, scaffolded instruction must be based on a continuous assessment of students' strengths and needs.

Throughout her career as an educator, Diane has been drawn to urban schools serving students of poverty who are often misunderstood, misdiagnosed, mistreated, and uncared for because of the unfamiliarity that exists between their families and their teachers. She established a high school student internship program between HSHMC and a neighborhood preK–6 school with a 95 percent population of English learners.

Diane has authored or edited dozens of books, articles, and speeches. As an educator, she has won numerous awards and, in 2005, was inducted into the International Reading Hall of Fame.

She earned a bachelor's degree from Ohio Northern University, a master's degree from Western Michigan University, and a doctorate from Indiana University–Bloomington.

To learn more about Diane's work, follow her on Twitter @lappsdsu.

Barbara Moss, PhD, is a professor at San Diego State University, where she teaches courses at the credential and master's levels. She has worked as an English or reading teacher at every grade level from 1–12 over the course of her career. She has also worked as a reading coach for teachers at both the elementary and secondary levels.

Barbara has specific expertise in the areas of disciplinary literacy, children's literature, and students' reading and writing of informational texts. She has published numerous articles in journals, including *The Reading Teacher*, the *Journal of Literacy Research*, *Reading and Writing Quarterly*, and *The California Reader*. She has authored and coauthored numerous books, including *A*

Close Look at Close Reading: Teaching Students to Analyze Complex Texts, Grades K–5 and *A Close Look at Close Reading: Teaching Students to Analyze Complex Texts, Grades 6–12* with Diane Lapp, Maria Grant, and Kelly Johnson.

Barbara earned her bachelor's degree and graduated summa cum laude from The Ohio State University and earned her master's and doctoral degrees from Kent State University.

Maria C. Grant, EdD, is a professor in secondary education at California State University, Fullerton (CSUF). She has authored numerous publications centered on science literacy, formative assessment, and reading and has written articles for *Educational Leadership* and the *Journal of Adolescent and Adult Literacy*. Additionally, she is coauthor of *Reading and Writing in Science: Tools to Develop Disciplinary Literacy* with Douglas Fisher and Diane Lapp.

Maria teaches courses in the credential and graduate programs at CSUF and conducts professional development with teachers at various schools across the United States. She is director of the Secondary Teacher Education Program and leads the Literacy Summer Seminar Series and the intern program at CSUF.

She earned a bachelor's degree in geological sciences at the University of California, Santa Barbara, a master's degree in curriculum and instruction at San Diego State University, and a doctorate from the joint doctoral program at the University of San Diego and San Diego State University.

Kelly Johnson, PhD, a National Board Certified teacher, is an instructional coach in the San Diego Unified School District, where she works with teachers, modeling best practices across the disciplines and grades. Kelly is also a faculty member in the school of teacher education at San Diego State University, where she teaches reading methods, classroom management, and liberal studies. Often referred to by her colleagues as a teacher's teacher, she has appeared in many instructional videos on teacher modeling, assessment and instruction, effective grouping, and writing instruction. Kelly's focus is on assessment and small-group instruction in secondary classrooms. She previously taught grades 1–6 and worked as a peer coach and a reading intervention teacher.

Kelly received the California Reading Association's Constance McCullough Research Award for her study on assessment and diagnostic instruction. She also received the International Reading Association's Celebrate Literacy Award, which honors educators for their significant literacy contributions. Kelly has published in *The Reading Teacher*, *The California Reader*, *The Reading Professor*, the *Journal of Adolescent and Adult Literacy*, and *Literacy*. She has also coauthored several books: *A Close Look at Close Reading: Teaching Students to Analyze Complex Texts, Grades K–5*; *A Close Look at Close Reading: Teaching Students to Analyze Complex Texts, Grades 6–12*; *Mining Complex Text: Using and Creating Graphic Organizers to Grasp Content and Share New Understandings, Grades*

6–12; *Accommodating Differences Among English Language Learners: Best Practices—75+ Literacy Lessons* (second and third [in press] editions); *Designing Responsive Curriculum: Planning Lessons That Work*; and *Teaching Literacy in First Grade*.

Kelly received a bachelor's degree from the University of California, San Diego, a master's degree from San Diego State University, and a doctorate from the joint program at Claremont Graduate University and San Diego State University.

To book Diane Lapp, Barbara Moss, Maria C. Grant, or Kelly Johnson for professional development, contact pd@SolutionTree.com.

Introduction

The educational landscape has been shifting ever since 2006, when an influential ACT (2006) study analyzed the reading abilities of 568,000 eighth, tenth, and twelfth graders on three reading tests and concluded that only 51 percent of twelfth graders were college ready. They noted, "students who can read complex texts are more likely to be ready for college. Those who cannot read complex texts are less likely to be ready for college" (p. 11). The alarm was sounded, and what resulted was the development of the Common Core State Standards (National Governors Association Center for Best Practices & Council of Chief State School Officers; NGA & CCSSO, 2010) and new state standards across the United States. These emphasized that students need to gain the skills and stamina to understand increasingly complex ideas shared in increasingly complex texts.

The National Governors Association Center for Best Practices and the Council of Chief State School Officers (n.d.a) note, "This finding is the impetus behind the Standards' strong emphasis on increasing text complexity as a key requirement in reading" (p. 2). This emphasis is also reflected in Next Generation Science Standards (NGSS Lead States, 2013) and the College, Career, and Civic Life (C3) Framework for Social Studies State Standards (National Council for the Social Studies; NCSS, 2013), which call for all students to be able to engage in evidence-based civic and scientific reasoning. Doing so involves gleaning, weaving, contrasting, and informing from many sources in order to make sound, well-documented arguments. This retrieving and sharing of information involves the literacy skills of reading, writing, and communicating.

We believe that all of these national and state frameworks and standards documents are in alignment, with the goal being to prepare students for college and career success, which is of course the intention of every teacher we know.

The reality is, the texts students read at all grade levels are much less complex than they need to be if students are to be college and career ready. College and career texts are at Lexile (L) levels around 1350. (See chapter 2 for a detailed discussion of Lexiles.) Eleventh and twelfth graders typically read materials at a Lexile measure of 1220, suggesting a gap of 130 points between the materials students read in high school and those they need to be able to read in college (Williamson, 2006). While student reading materials in grades 4 and higher have gotten easier over time (Adams, 2010–2011), college texts have become more difficult (Stenner, Koons, & Swartz, 2010). To close this text-complexity gap, new state and national standards recommend that students begin reading texts at higher Lexile measures in grades 2 and 3. Teachers are the critical factor in creating student success with these challenging complex texts; for students to read more complex texts, teachers will need to provide more and better instruction during close readings to ensure that every student will meet the state standards.

And what teacher wouldn't want to learn how to teach his or her students to closely read or think deeply about a complex text if that better prepares them for college and career experiences? Of course teachers want their students to be successful readers who love reading and are confident when taking on the challenging work of close reading. However, K–12 teachers are grappling with defining the term *close reading* and then attempting to develop instruction that enables all their students to gain proficiency with this practice. If you're reading this book, you might be like many teachers who have begun to engage students in the process of closely reading texts and are wondering what to do at the conclusion of the close reading experience when some students are unable to answer related text-dependent questions or engage in writing tasks that would indicate a high level of comprehension. You might even find yourself panicking after the initial reading as you wonder how to help all your students succeed with close reading. You might also be worried that teaching students to closely read texts could diminish their love of reading and their interest in self-selecting texts. Rest assured; you are not alone.

We, too, have asked what the next steps for each of our students should be after we've engaged them in close text reading. The short, quick answer is that the next instructional steps for each student must be scaffolded in ways that support his or her growing independence when reading increasingly complex texts. Close reading must be well balanced with other types of reading experiences, including guided reading, shared reading, and independent reading, with the goal being to produce proficient, independent readers who love to read. Close reading can also work in concert with independent reading. For example, effective teachers can engage students in reading interesting text excerpts that can provide a catalyst for students reading the entire book. A close reading can introduce readers to a compelling character, idea, or topic. This introduction can encourage students to read the entire book, which should be available to them in the classroom library. Learning how to closely read a text provides students with both motivation to take bigger risks as readers and the skills they need to succeed in their reading endeavors. They grow in independence because they know how to scrutinize textual information.

That all sounds great, but how exactly does it play out in real classrooms that may have anywhere from forty to ninety minutes available for close reading instruction and, in grades K–1, perhaps only fifteen to twenty minutes? Our intent in this book is to clarify exactly how you can differentiate the instruction that occurs during and after a close reading by identifying practical teaching strategies and scaffolds to create lessons that ensure success for every student. This book is intended to alleviate panicked feelings about what to do next after an initial reading by helping you understand how you can meaningfully identify individuals' strengths and needs and then design instructional scaffolds that enable every student to grow as a reader and learner.

Close Reading Instruction

The process of close text reading is so important to students' learning at all grade levels, and within all disciplines, that every teacher must address it. In fact, the National Governors Association Center for Best Practices (NGA) and the Council of Chief State School Officers (CCSSO) explain that, "Being able to read complex text independently and proficiently is essential for high achievement in college and the workplace and important in numerous life tasks" (NGA & CCSSO, n.d.a, p. 4). This proclamation has caused teachers to reaffirm their commitment to ensuring that no student slips through the cracks of reading instruction—unable to read well enough to be entertained, engage in a literary analysis, corroborate information from various historical sources, or classify and document information to support a claim.

Teaching students the practice of close reading can pay big dividends. The Partnership for Assessment of Readiness for College and Careers (PARCC, 2012), one of the assessment consortia for the NGA and CCSSO's Common Core State Standards (CCSS), notes that a

> significant body of research links the close reading of complex text—whether the student is a struggling reader or advanced—to significant gains in reading proficiency and finds close reading to be a key component of college and career readiness. (p. 7)

From our observations, most teachers agree that close reading can improve students' reading comprehension, but the deeper they get into the practice of close reading, the more they are asking what to do when it becomes obvious that texts within the grade-level band are too difficult for some students to successfully read. In prior years, we might have abandoned the original text, selected a less difficult one on the same topic, and felt secure in having those struggling students never return to the initial, more complex text. This can no longer be the case. We now must realize that this is as unacceptable as not providing every student the instruction that makes college a possible choice for them. Ensuring that students develop the language, communication, and reading skills needed to successfully read and discuss complex texts requires that teachers share a variety of instructional routines during a whole-class close reading. If some students do not initially have success reading the complex text, subsequent or contingent instruction must include the sharing of scaffolds that will move them toward a *continuous deepening* of their engagement with and comprehension of texts *at the upper levels of their grade bands*.

It is important to understand the general process around which we base this instruction. The practices we describe in this text are based on a rough progression that assumes the following. First, the teacher engages the whole class in an initial close reading of the text. There is no set number of times a text must be reread. The goal is that students investigate the text to identify its deepest meaning. This understanding generally occurs as students return to the text several times to answer questions their teachers pose that guide them to analyze the general meaning, language, structure, and author intent. During the whole-class close reading and related collaborative conversations, it may become apparent that students need to respond to additional questions regarding language or structure in order to support their comprehension. Rather than telling them or front-loading the information, the layered questions the teacher asks serve as scaffolds in order to help students dig deeper and deeper to access the text. The teacher differentiates the questions based on students' responses, which indicate how well they are comprehending the text. Based on the teacher's observation and assessment of student responses to these questions, the teacher will identify any students who still struggle to access the meaning of the text and will provide additional differentiated scaffolds to smaller groups of students until they gain the knowledge and understanding necessary to deeply comprehend the complex text. In this smaller group configuration teachers have twenty to thirty minutes to both support and stretch students who do not have initial success. These more intense differentiated scaffolds are known as *contingencies*, in that they are contingent on students' need for more focused scaffolding. When contingency scaffolds are implemented to support learning, they are a means of differentiation.

Scaffolds are the resources and instruction that students need from teachers in order to learn new concepts or complete a new task. Teachers choose these strategies or tools to support specific, identified needs of individual students. Some scaffolds occur during the whole-class close reading, while other contingent scaffolds may need to occur for a smaller group of students at the conclusion of the whole-class reading. We use classroom scenarios throughout the text to paint the picture of how this process plays out in various grade levels and disciplines and as a reference for how you can support students in your own classroom. Teachers can share scaffolds as questions, cues, prompts, and direct explanations (Fisher and Frey, 2014a).

Questions are the primary scaffold used during the whole-class close reading. These may consist of a next question, directing students to focus a bit more deeply on the language or structure of a specific passage, or to focus on a visual aspect in the material. This questioning can provide a hint by cueing the readers where to look for the needed information. A *prompt* reminds students of previous thinking that triggers a missing piece of information. After a whole-class close reading activity, smaller groups of students who have not deeply comprehended the text may need additional scaffolds, like *direct explanation,* that involve more detailed instruction.

The term *scaffold* was coined by Jerome Bruner (1966), who shared many of Lev Vygotsky's (1978) beliefs; Vygotsky describes what a student can do independently and with supports from an expert as the *zone of proximal development.* Teachers should remove scaffolds gradually as students gain the skills and proficiencies needed to function independently (Pearson & Gallagher, 1983). Independence in learning happens for students at different rates; some students may need only an initial scaffold, while others may need scaffolds throughout an entire lesson, and at the conclusion of the lesson there may still be a few students who need additional differentiated scaffolds before they become independent (Brush & Saye, 2002; Fisher & Frey, 2014a; Tharp, 1993).

Roland Tharp's (1993) plan for the management of scaffolds builds on Vygotsky's work and makes an allowance for a mismatch between the learner's actual zone of proximal development and the teacher's estimate of it. Tharp advocates for the use of contingencies when the initial scaffolds are not sufficient to support the learner. Thomas Brush and John Saye (2002) advance this work by talking about hard and soft scaffolds. *Hard scaffolds* are those the teacher plans while constructing the initial lesson. *Soft scaffolds* are those a teacher shares with individuals or smaller groups when he or she recognizes a need for them during or after the lesson. We, like our colleagues Douglas Fisher and Nancy Frey (2014b; Fisher, Frey, & Lapp, 2016), illustrate the use of soft, or contingent, scaffolds as subsequent scaffolds that are shared to differentiate instruction when the initial scaffolds are insufficient to promote the intended growth. We propose that contingent scaffolds be planned during the initial lesson construction so they will be at the teacher's fingertips if needed. This differentiated preparation is possible because teachers know their students well and can therefore anticipate in advance those who may need contingent scaffolds as they work individually, with partners, or in small-group configurations.

Deciding what scaffolds an individual or small group needs to succeed with a text involves a very close assessment of each student's performance while engaged in the close reading. This assessment begins by first asking yourself, What is causing this student to struggle with the text? or What information hasn't the student learned yet that is needed to support his or her comprehension of the text? Once you have the answer, you can plan appropriate next instruction. It is important to note that teachers should also invite students who have very good comprehension to participate in smaller-group scaffolded instruction on a regular basis. Every student deserves this very focused instruction to ensure they are becoming better and better at text analysis, and when small-group contingency instruction is a familiar and ordinary part of your grouping configuration, students do not view it negatively.

The ideas we share throughout this book are meant to help you gain skills in selecting complex texts and then plan both initial and next-step instructional scaffolds. The suggestions we offer assume that you have begun teaching your students how to closely read a selected text and now have new questions regarding how to ensure successful close reading for all students without damaging their love of reading. This book includes information and examples that we hope will alleviate your concerns.

Instructional Scenarios

Throughout this book, we include instructional scenarios spanning grades K–12 that illustrate teachers supporting students as they develop the ability to closely read a text. These scenarios model how to use formative assessment to plan for the initial close reading and then how to continue to support learning for all students, including those who are not initially successful. Success for students in each scenario occurs as teachers think about a text in relation to their students' abilities and note the areas that will be complex for them, including the author's use of language, discipline-specific vocabulary, layered levels of meaning, students' gaps in background knowledge, or an unfamiliar format or structure of the text. Once a teacher identifies the areas of complexity, he or she then decides how to address them and what text-dependent questions will cause students to carefully and deeply analyze the text. As students read and annotate the text, and partners discuss it, teachers can easily see how well students comprehend the text's deep meaning. By focusing on the thinking, planning, questioning, and instructional interventions the teachers in these scenarios use, you'll gain insights about formative assessment in action. With these insights, you can plan the next instructional steps that must occur for all students—those who had initial success with the text and also those who need to revisit the text or receive additional scaffolded instruction, perhaps in a smaller group.

As we've worked with colleagues in grades K–12, it has become obvious that the practice of close reading differs as one moves from the primary grades to the intermediate grades and beyond. While we realize that it is quite an undertaking to attempt to cover this grade-level span, we wanted to include primary grades because it is in these early years that young students learn to closely think about texts. This close thinking lays the groundwork for later close reading success. Students are simultaneously learning to decode and gain automaticity that will support their comprehension as they later read more deeply across disciplines and genres. In addition to elementary teachers, this is also a book for middle and high school science, social studies, music, art, and mathematics teachers who are considering how to support students as they read, write, and communicate about texts related to these disciplines. They are experts in their disciplines, and no one can teach a student how to read and communicate about science, history, mathematics, art, music, and technical subjects better than the teachers of these disciplines. In the middle and high school years, students read a myriad of text types throughout the school day. Because of these differences, we share close reading examples that highlight grade-level and disciplinary practices from scientists, historians, musicians, artists, and mathematicians as well as rhetoricians.

In these scenarios, we'll share a plan that involves:

- **Selecting** an appropriately complex text that supports an identified learning target
- **Identifying** the areas of complexity as related to the students who will be reading the text
- **Realizing** that these areas of complexity are exactly where instruction is needed—these are the teaching points or areas needing instructional focus
- **Creating** text-dependent questions that focus attention on what the text says, how it works, and what it means
- **Introducing** the text without front-loading the vocabulary and concepts
- **Observing** students as they engage with reading, annotating, and talking about the text in response to the questions the teacher asks
- **Assessing** who is comprehending the original text and who isn't
- **Identifying** what is causing a student to have difficulty with the text
- **Planning** the scaffolds that will further support *each* student's extended learning
- **Teaching** in ways that promote extended learning for each student

For your convenience, appendix A (page 151) identifies the grade-level instructional scenarios shared in this text, where to find each, and the instructional focus that is being emphasized.

To support your teaching, we also provide tools to help you identify areas of complexity in a text and to record students' behavior and responses as they read the text. (Visit **go.SolutionTree.com/literacy** to access material related to this book.) We illustrate how to use each tool while planning and observing close reading. At first glance, you might feel that using these tools is complex. We felt exactly the same way when we began using them, but through the examples we've included, our goal is to illustrate that while your initial apprehension is warranted, close reading—like any other instructional approach you've implemented—grows less complex as you become familiar with it. To support you, we've also included ideas regarding the next steps for instruction for all your students—those who initially succeed and those needing a bit more instruction. Our goal is to support your instruction as you engage all your students in purposeful tasks that promote their increasing proficiency in close reading and in using information they learned from their reading to create new understanding.

Overview of Chapters

To support teachers at every grade level and discipline, we begin this text with a review of what's involved for readers and their teachers during a close reading. We have wrestled with close reading as we have taught it to students and as we have discussed the approach of close text reading with colleagues at all grade levels and in all disciplines. Based on these collective insights, we offer a plan for what we've found works best for our students during and after close reading.

We also review how to identify the complex areas of a text and then how to ask text-dependent layered questions that support students interrogating the text. Since close reading is often initially a whole-class activity that involves all students reading the same text, we ask what happens when some students are unable to successfully read the text. To answer this question, we share instructional scenarios illustrating how teachers first identify the problem areas causing confusion for the student and then how they make the text more accessible through word work, focused rereading, analysis of the layers of the text, and targeted discussion that occurs within both whole-group and small-group configurations.

Throughout the text, we emphasize that you will have to design differentiated scaffolds for many students who may not arrive at the deepest meaning of a text at the same rate as their peers. Because of limitations in background knowledge, language, and other skills, some students may need a bit more support than can be provided through the initial question scaffolds regarding the text's meaning, language, structure, and knowledge demands. They may need additional or contingency scaffolds to support their analysis of the text. We believe that with very focused differentiated scaffolds these students will be able to read the initial complex text and participate in related extension tasks.

Part I of this text offers chapters that define close reading and text complexity and outline the foundational components of crafting lessons centered around these areas.

In chapter 1, we share a definition of close reading that we believe illustrates that teachers at all grade levels and of all disciplines must teach all students the practice of close reading. We also emphasize the skills readers need to employ during a close reading. In chapter 2, we identify why students need to read complex texts, and we define and illustrate the features that make a text complex. We share rubrics that will help you identify areas of text complexity, teaching points to support your students' proficiency, and a checklist for evaluating reader and task aspects of complexity. In this chapter, we examine exemplar texts and what may cause them to be complex for your students. Chapter 3 addresses in detail the decisions you will need to make from the time you initially decide to add close reading to your curriculum. Each decision can also serve as a self-assessment of your developing understanding of the close reading approach and yourself as a teacher who is able to equip students with this skill. We note in chapter 4 that continuous assessment is the foundation of close reading instruction and provide a detailed example illustrating how assessment that is focused on student performance is essential to ensure that all students learn to closely read complex texts.

In part II of this text, we provide examples of instructional contingencies that we believe will make close reading success a reality for every student, as well as several close reading lesson exemplars illustrating how every student can be supported to become a reader of complex texts. These differentiated scaffolds are designed to support students who, at the conclusion of the close reading, still need additional support to comprehend the complex text. Whole- and small-group participation and classroom management are also featured. These scenarios and the students and teachers featured in them are fictional composites based on our personal teaching experiences and our work in the classrooms of many colleagues.

More specifically, chapter 5 provides examples of differentiated scaffolds that support students developing an understanding of the text's general meaning. Chapter 6 provides examples of differentiated scaffolds that support students' understanding of text organization and structure. Chapter 7 identifies examples of differentiated scaffolds that support students developing needed academic and topical language. Chapter 8 identifies differentiated scaffolds that prepare students to acquire the depth of background knowledge the text demands.

As we suggest throughout this text, close reading is definitely an approach to text analysis that every student can learn and apply as he or she reads texts within his or her grade-level bands. Watch your students and, based on their behaviors, you'll be able to determine the initial instructional scaffolds and later contingency scaffolds to provide to help each succeed. The examples shared throughout this book will support you in designing close reading instruction that promotes deep reading of complex texts for all students.

PART I

BACKGROUND AND
PLANNING INFORMATION

Part I is designed to ensure that readers of this text have a common understanding of what's involved in planning and implementing a close reading of a complex text. To support this understanding, we clarify definitions of key terms and concepts and establish the foundational knowledge needed to plan and implement close reading of complex texts for students within the same class who have varying levels of understanding and diverse learning needs. After establishing a shared understanding of concepts and terms, we examine considerations for implementation and assessment.

1

Understanding
Close Reading

What constitutes a close reading, and what types of instruction support close reading? These are two questions that many educators have considered since 2010 when NGA and CCSSO's (2010) Common Core State Standards identified the ability to "read closely to determine what the text says explicitly and to make logical inferences from it; cite specific textual evidence when writing or speaking to support conclusions drawn from the text" as the first English language arts anchor standard for reading (p. 10). *Anchor standards* are the overarching expectations of the CCSS for each of the four strands: Reading, Writing, Speaking and Listening, and Language. As more and more teachers become comfortable crafting instruction and management that support close reading across grades and disciplines, many wonder what to do at the end of a close reading when some students are still struggling to understand the text and also what to do with those who have mastered the text.

To begin to explore answers to these questions, we first need a shared definition of close reading. Sheila Brown and Lee Kappes (2012) provide a comprehensive description:

> Close Reading of text involves an investigation of a short piece of text, with multiple readings done over multiple instructional lessons. Through text-based questions and discussion, students are guided to deeply analyze and appreciate various aspects of the text, such as key vocabulary and how its meaning is shaped by context; attention to form, tone, imagery and/or rhetorical devices; the significance of word choice and syntax; and the discovery of different levels of meaning as passages are read multiple times. . . . Close Reading cannot be reserved for students who already are strong readers; it should be a vehicle through which all students grapple with advanced concepts and participate in engaging discussions regardless of their independent reading level. (p. 2)

We especially like their definition because it includes every student. We would add that while this deep comprehension of text may not happen for all students by the end of the whole-class close reading, it still needs to happen. To ensure success for all, teachers may need to add smaller group instruction to the instructional plan.

A History of Close Reading

As educators add close reading to their instructional practice toolbox, many are wondering if it is a new practice. The answer is no. Close reading has a long history and tradition, with roots in the New Criticism of the 1920s and 1930s, which demanded a tight, clear, analytical reading of a text, especially short stories and poems. Emphasis was on understanding the explicit meaning of the text, which was to be acquired through a deep, probing analysis that resulted from reading and rereading. This close reading required readers to "x-ray" the book to locate the deep structures of several features within the text in order to arrive at its meaning (Adler & Van Doren, 1972). This model focused on analysis of language patterns, with particular attention being paid to literary techniques like irony, paradox, and symbolism (Hinchman & Moore, 2013). The emphasis on language form, referred to as a *formalist* approach to literary understanding, was a reaction to earlier approaches that emphasized the study of the text in relation to its author, historical time frame, politics, and other considerations external to the text itself. Theorists like I.A. Richards (1929) emphasized the need to identify the one "correct" meaning of the text. It's interesting to note that the idea of having students identify the one correct interpretation characterized the instruction occurring in English language arts classrooms in the 1950s and 1960s.

As time went on, different approaches to close reading gained prominence. By the 1970s, for example, reader-response theories (Rosenblatt, 1978) dominated English language arts, moving the emphasis from the text itself to the reader's transaction with the text, which was based on the reader's own experiences. This approach de-emphasized the view that a text contained a single correct meaning; instead, the approach emphasized the interplay between the individual reader's experiences and the text itself. Classroom instruction paralleled this model, and readers were encouraged to make text-to-self connections.

CCSS and other new state standards have shifted the emphasis from reader-response approaches back to close, interpretive reading of complex texts. The standards de-emphasize instructional practices such as activating prior knowledge, making predictions, and making personal connections to the text. The emphasis is on focusing readers' attention more closely, instead, on the content found on the page, specifically focusing understanding at three different levels of meaning: (1) what the text says, (2) how the text works, and (3) what the text, at its deepest level, means (Kurland, n.d.). This does not mean that students do not use prior knowledge and make personal connections when they read; it is just that these areas are not emphasized instructionally as much during close reading.

When students read closely to consider what the text *says*, they are reading to get the gist of the text by restating information that illustrates their general understanding. As they read closely to consider how the text *works*, they will think about how the author constructs the text, considering whether he or she uses examples or particular structures or the kinds of arguments or language he or she uses. At the deepest level of comprehension, students read closely to consider what the text *means*. At this point, the reader creates an interpretation of the text; readers infer the larger meaning of the text that can be supported from information found within the text.

Research Supporting the Power of Close Reading

According to P. David Pearson (2013), the CCSS are firmly based in cognitive research, particularly in terms of Walter Kintsch's (1998) construction-integration model. Kintsch's construction-integration model of reading processing identifies two levels of representation: (1) the text base and (2) the situation model. As we think about this model, consider the types of comprehension required at each level during a close reading.

The Text Base: What the Text Says and How It Works

Text-based comprehension demands that readers accurately read the text to answer the fundamental question, What does the text say?, and store this information in short-term memory.

The three CCSS Reading anchor standards within the Key Ideas and Details domain (reading closely to determine what the text says explicitly, determining central ideas, and developing ideas over the course of a text) are especially pertinent to reconstructing the text base (Pearson, 2013). Comprehension at this text-based level is focused on an accurate, mainly literal, understanding of the text. To create this understanding, readers need to determine central ideas and note their development. Their comprehension does not occur in a vacuum; readers will naturally use their prior knowledge as they reconstruct the text's meaning. To understand this, let's consider the following sentences.

- Mary wanted to become a concert violinist.
- She practiced her violin for four hours each day.

To connect the meaning of these two sentences, the reader uses prior knowledge to connect the name *Mary* with the pronoun *she* and to infer the relationship between the two sentences. In addition, in constructing the meaning of this text the reader also considers the question, How does the text work? In other words, the reader thinks about how the author has created the text. In order to ascertain a text structure (anchor standard five) or evaluate an argument (anchor standard eight) readers must possess basic understanding of the text's message (Pearson, 2013).

The Situation Model: What the Text Means

The situation model is the second level of representation in the construction-integration model. This level focuses on what the text means. It involves the reader in maintaining text-based understanding and consistency in the prior knowledge that has been previously activated (Pearson, 2013). With this model, readers rely more on prior knowledge and inference. With the previous example about Mary, readers might use their background knowledge to infer that Mary has a challenging task before her, since not everyone can become a concert violinist. They might also infer that Mary is highly motivated and goes after what she wants, since she is willing to work hard to achieve her goal. This construction of a situation model is central to comprehension because it lets readers integrate their prior knowledge with what they read as well as build new knowledge structures that may enhance or replace those in long-term memory. Common Core Reading anchor standards one through three address this model through references to terms like *analyze*, *summarize*, *develop*, and *interact*, as do anchor standards four (*interpret words and phrases*), six (*assess point of view*), seven (*integrate and evaluate content*), and nine (*compare texts*) (Pearson, 2013).

Instruction is central to success with close reading. If students are to meet identified anchor standards, they need quality instruction. For students to closely read to know what the text says, how it works, and what it means, it is essential that teachers continually assess student performance and, using this information, provide scaffolded and contingent instruction to support their learning.

Close Reading Across All Grades and Disciplines

As noted in the introduction to this book, close reading in the elementary grades differs from that in the middle and upper grades. The major difference is that when engaging primary-grades students in close reading, the teacher reads the text aloud to the students. Even at this early age, students can be engaged in deep thinking about the text and in partner conversations that push their understanding. Questions should be appropriate for the students' cognitive level. Even young readers need to learn to struggle a bit to succeed with comprehension if asked an appropriate question. Just as with close reading at all other grade levels, you will want to begin by explaining the lesson purpose, for example, to identify the traits of a character in a story or to identify the main idea in an informational text. Just as in the later grades, it will be important to have students support their thinking with text-based information. Initially, because of the questions the teacher asks, he or she directs the process of close reading. As students become skilled with this approach, they gain the independence to individually tackle increasingly complex texts.

Let us be clear that close reading in the primary grades is not meant to replace the teaching of phonics or foundational skills. Close reading should not occur in the leveled books teachers use for guided reading because most of these texts are not complex enough to warrant a close reading. We are not suggesting that leveled texts should not be part of a literacy program but rather that they should not be the texts selected for close reading. Close reading should occur as a shared reading and thinking experience in the primary grades. In addition, instruction to develop foundational skills should and must also occur if students are to gain reading fluency and automaticity. In fact, the *Common Core State Standards for English Language Arts and Literacy in History/Social Studies, Science, and*

Technical Subjects (NGA & CCSSO, 2010) identifies the need to develop foundational reading skills in grades K–5:

> These standards address fostering students' understanding and working knowledge of concepts of print, the alphabetic principle, and other basic conventions of the English writing system. These foundational skills are not an end in and of themselves; rather, they are necessary and important components of an effective, comprehensive reading program designed to develop proficient readers with the capacity to comprehend texts across a range of types and disciplines. (NGA & CCSSO, 2010, p. 15)

Strong readers will need much less practice with these concepts than struggling readers will, which means that effective teachers will differentiate instruction to meet students where they are in terms of these foundational skills. As the CCSS for English language arts note, "The point is to teach students what they need to learn and not what they already know—to discern when particular children or activities warrant more or less attention" (NGA & CCSSO, 2010, p. 15). Foundational skills are essential to comprehension and are acquired at different rates.

While the process of close text reading remains similar across grades and disciplines, what changes is the type of text that is being read. During social studies, students can closely read primary and secondary sources, photos, or other historical artifacts such as stories, diaries, and paintings. In science class, students often closely read to make observations, investigate phenomena, identify and describe specimens, and create graphic organizers of their data (Lapp, Grant, Moss, & Johnson, 2013). Students can closely read a problem in mathematics or a score in music. In health and physical education, texts and diagrams often need detailed analysis. In language arts or English classrooms, students closely read to critique a lecture or analyze a poem, a speech, or a play. While the text may change, the purpose of close reading remains the same—for students to gain understanding of a text, regardless of its type.

Conclusion

As we highlight throughout this text, students, regardless of grade, may have different levels of comprehension at the conclusion of a close reading. As with any other process you have taught, students will gain proficiency at different rates. Some may be ready to move independently to apply the newly acquired information, while others may need additional time with you revisiting the text to unlock its deepest meaning.

Your goal must be to ensure that all students do, however, gain this proficiency. Across the disciplines, the key to close reading is that regardless of genre, you should select texts that are sufficiently challenging and support students in learning how to read them. In the next chapter, we'll examine the process of selecting appropriately challenging texts for your students.

2 Identifying Text Complexity

Daily, ongoing practice in closely reading progressively more challenging texts strengthens students' reading muscles and equips them to read more deeply. Having students spend most of their time reading comfort-level texts fails to challenge them. Teachers will want to ramp up text difficulty in ways that will help students read appropriately complex texts independently by the end of each school year, as required by anchor standard ten for reading. More specifically, the International Literacy Association (formerly the International Reading Association) guidelines for Common Core implementation (International Reading Association, n.d.) note that students in grades K and 1 should engage with complex texts through teacher read-alouds, and students in grades 2–12 should be given opportunities to read complex texts. At least some of these texts should require students to struggle in ways that help them develop persistence and stamina, two characteristics of good readers.

What does this mean for your students? It means they will read more challenging complex texts more often and more closely and deeply than in the past (Lapp, Moss, Grant, & Johnson, 2015). According to PARCC (2012), research links close reading of complex texts to gains in reading proficiency for all readers—whether struggling or advanced.

Whether you realize it or not, as an accomplished reader, you are aware of text complexity. Even more, as a teacher, you are always considering text complexity as you think about engaging your students in reading particular books in each discipline. One of this book's authors, Barb, just finished reading the 2014 Newbery Medal winner, *Flora and Ulysses: The Illuminated Adventures* (DiCamillo, 2013), a graphic novel featuring a zany adventure story full of quirky characters, including a flying squirrel with superhero powers. The book's audience is approximately third graders, and as she read the book, Barb informally considered how well the book would work with these students by creating a mental checklist as she read.

- Are there interesting characters?
- Are the relationships between characters easily understood?
- Is the plot easy to follow?

- Is the text too long?
- Is the text written in a kid-friendly style?
- Are there short sentences?
- Is the theme easy to identify?
- Is minimal background knowledge required?
- Is the vocabulary easy to understand?

As she read the book, one key factor stood out: the author's choice of vocabulary. *Flora and Ulysses* is full of sophisticated words and phrases that would challenge most third graders. For example, the text was riddled with phrases like "holy unanticipated consequences," "port in a storm," "an extended hallucination," and many more.

When more formally evaluating the book's complexity, Barb evaluated quantitative features like the number of words in the sentences, qualitative features like the book's structure, style, and language, and the book in relation to the third graders who would read it—the reader and task factors.

To get started with close reading, teachers need to identify potential texts for classroom use. These texts should be short, worthy texts with deep and rich content suitable for multiple readings. The texts should be ones that introduce new ideas and concepts and build knowledge in the reader (Wixson & Valencia, 2014). They should engage students in reading a variety of genres and address disciplinary content in subject areas like social science, English language arts, science, and mathematics. In selecting texts, remember that "rigor is not an attribute of the text but rather a characteristic of our behavior with that text" (Beers & Probst, 2013, p. 20). Text complexity is based on three factors: (1) quantitative features, (2) qualitative features, and (3) reader and task factors. In the following sections, we discuss how teachers can evaluate texts across the grades and disciplines for quantitative features, qualitative features, and reader and task factors.

Quantitative Features

Quantitative features of text complexity that a computer program can count include sentence length, number of syllables, word length, word frequency, and other quantifiable features. Different formulas measure different aspects of complexity. The Advantage/ TASA Open Standard (ATOS) text analyzer and Degrees of Reading Power (DRP) are two well-known computer programs that measure text complexity. In addition, Lexiles are often the readability formula of choice for measuring quantitative features of texts. Lexile text measures are based on factors like word frequency and sentence length and rank texts based on a number from 0L to above 2000L. (See www.lexile.com to learn more about Lexiles, and visit **go.SolutionTree.com/literacy** to access live links to the websites mentioned in this book.)

Lexile ranges of texts for different grade levels include stretch texts designed to keep students on track for reading texts of increasing complexity by the time they finish high school, or to prepare them for college and career readiness (CCR). (See table 2.1.) Examples of complex texts can be found in appendix B of the CCSS, which notes that students need to read texts at these stretch levels if they are to be able to ultimately read college and career materials successfully (NGA & CCSSO, n.d.b). Additional text examples are available in appendix D of *Teaching Tolerance* (2015), on the Teaching Tolerance website (www.tolerance.org/classroom-resources), and on the website Teach the Books You Love (http://ttbyl.net).

Table 2.1: Stretch Lexile Bands for Grades K-12

Grade Band	Current Lexile Band	Stretch Lexile Band
K–1	N/A	N/A
2–3	450L–730L	420L–820L
4–5	640L–850L	740L–1010L
6–8	860L–1010L	925L–1185L
9–10	960L–1120L	1050L–1335L
11–CCR	1070L–1220L	1185L–1385L

Lexile measures, however, provide only a part of the text-complexity picture; qualitative text features help complete the picture.

Qualitative Features

Qualitative features can't be measured with a number. They require teachers to carefully analyze texts on a variety of dimensions. Because the knowledge, language, and skills a reader brings to the task affect the text complexity, as you conduct this analysis, always be thinking about the students who will be reading the texts.

PARCC (2012) notes that:

> Close, analytic reading stresses engaging with a text of sufficient complexity directly and examining its meaning thoroughly and methodically, encouraging students to read and reread deliberately. Directing student attention on the text itself empowers students to understand the central ideas and key supporting details. It also enables students to reflect on the meanings of individual words and sentences; the order in which sentences unfold; and the development of ideas over the course of the text, which ultimately leads students to arrive at an understanding of the text as a whole. (p. 7)

To achieve this, it follows, as noted in chapter 1, that there are three key questions teachers should consider carefully in terms of their students' abilities to comprehend a given text: (1) What does the text say?, (2) How does the text work?, and (3) What does the text mean? In addition, we have identified four key dimensions of student comprehension that relate to each question and several aspects for consideration that comprise each dimension. Dimensions 1–3 correspond respectively with these three questions. The fourth dimension, knowledge demands, is overarching and relates to each of these questions.

- **Dimension 1:** Understanding the general meaning of the text
    - Main ideas
    - Key details
- **Dimension 2:** Understanding the workings of the text
    - Organization
    - Visual supports and layout
    - Relationships among ideas
    - Vocabulary
    - Author's purpose
- **Dimension 3:** Understanding the deep meaning of the text
    - Author's style and tone
    - Theme
    - Point of view
    - Uses of language
    - Language register
- **Dimension 4:** Meeting knowledge demands
    - Background knowledge (experiential, topical, cultural, literary)

What the text says involves assessing students' understanding of the general meaning of the text (dimension 1), especially main ideas and details. How the text works involves assessing students' understanding of the workings of the text (dimension 2). This dimension includes organization, visual supports, layouts, relationships among ideas, vocabulary, and author's purpose. To consider what the text means, the reader must stretch beyond basic understanding and recognition of the author's craft to understand the deep meaning of the text (dimension 3), which includes analysis of the author's style and tone, theme, point of view, uses of language, and language register. Meeting knowledge demands (dimension 4) ensures students have the contextual information necessary to achieve deep understanding of the text. Teachers need to evaluate each dimension in relation to the students who will read the text in order to analyze the areas that may interfere with students' comprehension, whether they are reading narrative or informational texts.

What the Text Says

Before they can dig deeply into a text, students need to have a general understanding of what the text says. Considerations within this dimension include main ideas and key details, which address student understanding of what the text says. Whether a text is narrative or informational, its meaning may be obvious and easily identified, or it may be subtle and appreciated on a variety of levels.

Fundamental understanding of what a text says requires comprehension of the author's main ideas and key details, which range from explicitly stated to inferred. The ability to identify the big ideas in a text, along with the details that develop that idea, is essential for reading both literary and informational texts. From first graders grappling with the main ideas and details of a simple story to twelfth graders grappling with the major concepts in a complex Shakespearean drama, this ability is central to the reading enterprise.

How the Text Works

Text comprehension also involves students understanding how the text is put together; in other words, how the author has chosen to craft her or his message. The dimension of how the text works includes five areas: (1) organization, (2) visual supports and layout, (3) relationships among ideas, (4) vocabulary, and (5) author's purpose. These matters differ depending on whether the text is narrative or informational.

Organization

Narrative texts' organizational patterns take different forms; some contain plots that are simple and chronological, while others move back and forth in time. In narrative books like *Esperanza Rising* (Ryan, 2000), the author uses a mostly, but not entirely, chronological structure, with chapter titles representing key times of the year during which workers harvest specific fruits or vegetables on the farm where the protagonist works. More sophisticated young adult novels like *Strings Attached* (Blundell, 2011), a story of an aspiring teen actress in New York in the 1950s, require readers to understand shifts in time and place over the course of the story. These are denoted by dates at the top of the page but are easy for readers to miss.

Informational texts may be organized using one or more expository structures, which include sequence, description, compare and contrast, cause and effect, and problem and solution.

- **Sequence:** Language conveying sequence describes items or events in order. It may also identify the steps to follow in a procedure or task. Sequence language can be simple (*first, second, next, last*) or it can be more academic, more subtle, and more sophisticated (*initially, consecutively, furthermore, ultimately, after*). Teaching students to identify words that indicate sequence can help them unlock meaning about a procedure or task.

- **Description:** Descriptive language involves terms and phrases that indicate features, characteristics, or examples of a topic, person, place, thing, or idea. Phrases that signal description include *such as, an example, to illustrate,* and *characteristics include.* Understanding such phrases helps readers to understand what things look like, how they function, or what's important to notice.

- **Compare and contrast:** Language showing a compare-and-contrast relationship illustrates how two or more things are similar and different. Words that signal compare and contrast include *in comparison, to contrast, when comparing, similarly, contrastingly, on the other hand, both,* and *as opposed to.* Identification of this language helps readers to identify commonalities and variances between ideas, objects, issues, and other things.

- **Cause and effect:** Cause-and-effect language indicates why something happened (*cause*) and what happened (*effect*). Indicators for this type of text structure can be simple words (*so, because, since, therefore*) or they can be longer phrases that connect one or more sentence ideas (*this led to, as a result, due to, if . . . then*). Readers who can skillfully notice cause-and-effect language are better able to comprehend relationships between an occurrence and a corresponding result.

- **Problem and solution:** Problem-and-solution language notes a problem and a corresponding remedy. Terms that indicate problem-and-solution text structure include *the dilemma is, the question is, to solve this, one suggestion,* and *an answer could be.* Readers who notice such language are better able to explore, critique, and evaluate issues via possible solutions.

More complex texts often contain more than one type of expository structure, while simpler ones may contain only one structure. For example, in her seminal book *Silent Spring*, Rachel Carson (1962) employs both cause-and-effect and problem-and-solution text structures to discuss how the pesticide DDT can infiltrate the food chain to cause irrevocable damage to all creatures, from birds to humans. She presents a potential outcome—one that is bleak—if harmful chemical use were to be continued. In this manner, Carson moves from an analysis of the current situation to a prediction of the possible outcomes if status quo use of pesticides is maintained. Clearly such a move in writing presents text complexity that requires deep critical thinking and analysis. An understanding of how such text structures are used in science writing, as a means to convey research and associated ideas, is essential.

Visual Supports and Layout

In informational texts, the many maps, graphs, charts, and diagrams can be essential to supporting the reader's understanding, but can also be very complex. *The Great Fire* (Murphy, 2010), for example, traces the progress of the horrific Chicago fire of 1871 across the city and its impact on the residents. The many maps in this informational book illustrate the progress of the fire over time. They provide crucial visual information that clarifies the reader's understanding of the text. Layout features like font, type size, and column arrangement also affect complexity in both narrative and informational texts. In Kevin Henkes's (1996) fictional picture book *Lilly's Purple Plastic Purse*, the artist uses a traditional text font to tell the story, along with capitalized text within speech bubbles to show what different characters in the illustrations are thinking and saying. Narrative texts for older readers, however, typically include few or no visual supports, with the exception of graphic novels, whose visual format is integral to the story being told.

Relationships Among Ideas

These can be simple or complicated. In a narrative text, relationships among characters or plots and subplots can be quite clear and simple or extremely complex and confusing. Most narrative books for beginning readers, like the *Henry and Mudge* stories (Rylant, 1987–2007), contain straightforward and simple relationships among key characters. Narratives and plays for older readers often contain complex and subtle relationships among characters. In Shakespearean plays like *Romeo and Juliet*, for example, keeping track of large numbers of characters and their relationships with one another creates challenges for the best of readers.

In informational texts, relationships among main ideas, facts, and details are essential for comprehension since they often weave a web of ideas that span an entire article or text. In Larry Dane Brimner's (2014) *Strike! The Farm Workers' Fight for Their Rights*, for example, the reader needs to see the relationship among a number of key ideas just within the first chapter. The author opens the book by describing the 1965 strike among Filipino migrant workers in Delano, California, then traces the history of their efforts and the ongoing violence between farm workers and strikebreakers, and then details the state government's response to the strike, along with that of the Mexican farm workers. The chapter concludes with the introduction of Cesar Chavez and his fledgling organization, the National Farm Workers Association (now United Farm Workers of America), and describes how Filipino farm workers forged an alliance with this organization. To fully understand this chapter, the reader needs to see the relationships among the ideas presented to realize how events converged to link the Filipino farm workers with the larger organization and its associated movement.

Vocabulary

Vocabulary considerations are essential to text understanding for both narrative and expository texts. In narrative texts, context clues can often aid readers in figuring out meanings of unknown words, while in informational texts the domain-specific nature of vocabulary can create unique challenges for students. The book *Flora and Ulysses: The Illuminated Adventures* (DiCamillo, 2013), which we will discuss in depth later in this chapter, is an exemplar of the ways in which challenging vocabulary can stymie readers, even in books that are otherwise not terribly complex.

In informational texts, comprehension of academic vocabulary unique to a discipline is essential to reader success. In *Molecules: The Elements and the Architecture of Everything*, author Theodore Gray (2014) necessarily incorporates numerous domain-specific terms including the words *nucleus*, *orbitals*, and *electrostatic force*. These terms are sprinkled between words like *ethylene*, *benzene*, and other equally challenging and specialized terms. As the reader progresses through the text, more words are added to the growing bank of complex terms. A reader who struggles with acquiring such terminology or who is unaware of best practices for negotiating complex vocabulary might be impelled to quit reading. Needed perseverance is dependent on the efficacy that results from knowing how to tackle readings that are rich in domain-specific vocabulary.

Author's Purpose

Authors have an array of purposes for the books they craft. Purposes of narrative texts are as varied as their authors; authors may elect to reveal a character's life during a particular period in history, such as in the young adult story of a friendship between a World War II pilot and a British spy in *Code Name Verity* (Wein, 2012). While the author's purpose is clearly to tell a compelling story, another purpose could be to describe the historical backdrop of the time period.

Informational texts usually include one of five purposes: to instruct, recount, explain, describe, or persuade. *Sunken Treasure* (Gibbons, 1988) is an informational picture book that effectively uses description and explanation to detail the discovery of the 1622 Spanish galleon ship *The Atocha* at the bottom of the ocean. It carefully describes the search, the discovery, the recovery, and the artifacts the ship yielded, including a priceless treasure of gold coins, precious jewels, and an astrolabe of incalculable value.

What the Text Means

Determining the deeper meaning of the text pushes readers beyond cursory, surface-level understanding to deeper inferential, analytic comprehension. For example, one can read the fantasy story *The Lion, the Witch, and the Wardrobe* (Lewis, 2005) as an enjoyable story of a fantasy quest or, on a deeper level, as an allegory in which the character Aslan represents Christ and the story line incorporates an allusion to the Christian resurrection.

What the text means includes five considerations: (1) the author's style and tone, (2) theme, (3) point of view, (4) uses of language, and (5) language register, all of which require students to think deeply about what a text means rather than simply focusing on main idea and key details.

Style and Tone

Good authors make decisions about their writing based on the story or information they want to tell. These decisions typically influence the style and tone of the story or informational text. In the biographical picture book *Duke Ellington: The Piano Prince and His Orchestra*, for example, Andrea Davis Pinkney (2006) adopts a slang-filled jazzy style and breezy tone to relate the life story of this jazz great. The book opens with this sentence, which illustrates Pinkney's style and tone: "You ever hear of the jazz-playin' man, the man with the cats who could swing with his band?" (p. 6). Tone and style are also critical components of informational texts. Expository texts that convey information are usually formal in tone, using third person and passive voice, similar to how information is presented in an encyclopedia. In Gail Gibbons's (1994) *Nature's Green Umbrella: Tropical Rain Forests*, for example, the author primarily uses this tone. In describing the rain forest she states: "Although a rain forest is one ecosystem, it is made up of different layers. In each layer, the plants and animals are specially suited to their place in the ecosystem." Literary nonfiction, which includes the Duke Ellington biography, may employ a more conversational tone.

Theme

The theme represents the message the author wants the reader to take away from the text. A key theme of the informational book *Imprisoned: The Betrayal of Japanese Americans During World War II* (Sandler, 2013) is the unfairness of Japanese Americans' internment and their resilience during the war. *Under the Blood-Red Sun* (Salisbury, 1994), a young adult historical fiction book about the same topic, contains a similar theme about the power of the human spirit to transcend unfairness and adversity.

Point of View

Part of the author's craft is to determine the point of view from which the story will be told. The narration can take the form of first, second, or third person. In still other instances, multiple points of view occur within the same book. In *Code Name Verity* (Wein, 2012), the first half of the story is told from the point of view of the spy (code name: Verity), and the second half is told by the pilot, Maddie. Varied points of view are also found in books that describe historical events. In *Crossing the Delaware: A History in Many Voices*, author Louise Peacock (2007) recounts the story of General George Washington crossing the Delaware, using multiple voices: a present-day narrator, the letters of a fictional soldier, and true accounts from the time.

Uses of Language

In a narrative text, descriptive language and literary devices like metaphors, similes, onomatopoeia, and others can challenge student understanding. Poets often use such figurative language in their work, which frequently results in students complaining "Poetry is hard!" "I just don't get it!" or "What in the world is he trying to say?!" For example, in Emily Dickinson's "In a Library" (Lisa, 2011), high school students may not be able to understand why Dickinson would use personification to assist with imagery and emotion and make a connection with the reader. In fact, some students may even struggle to identify the personification used, such as in the lines "To meet an antique book, / In just the dress his century wore" (2–3) and "Old volumes shake their vellum heads" (27). Additionally, students may not be able to locate where Dickinson uses metaphors and what objects are being compared.

Texts that combine narrative elements with information, called *literary nonfiction*, use literary devices combined with facts to create vivid pictures in readers' minds. In *Starfish* (Hurd, 2000), a literary nonfiction book for young children, the author uses alliteration, metaphors, and similes to illustrate starfish behaviors. For example, "Starfish have feet, but no toes. They glide and slide on tiny tube feet. They move as slowly as a snail" (p. 10). Within these few sentences, the author uses three literary devices: rhyme ("glide and slide"), alliteration ("tiny tube"), and simile ("as slowly as a snail").

With traditional informational text formats, like encyclopedia entries or textbooks, authors use discipline-related language constructions such as if . . . then, cause and effect, and other constructions unique to science. For example, in *Ocean: The Definitive Visual Guide* (American Museum of Natural History, 2014) the author writes about earthquakes and stress buildup, stating, "When this happens, a huge amount of energy can be released in a short time" (p. 49). Later in the text, the author notes, "A tsunami may be triggered if an earthquake results in the uplift or subsidence of part of the seafloor" (p. 49). Clearly a familiarity with the common language construction of cause and effect is needed when reading science texts. Proficient science readers know that there are conditions that effect changes and determine outcomes. Signal words such as *if . . . then, when, consequently, as a result, therefore, because, since,* and *this led to* indicate to the reader that particular conditions, circumstances, or events have effects or outcomes. Proficient readers know how to follow these leads to incorporate cause-and-effect thinking into the constructs they are developing as a result of their reading.

Language Register

Reading texts written in forms other than standard English can pose unique challenges for both narrative and informational text readers. The colloquial language found in Mark Twain's (1994) classic *The Adventures of Huckleberry Finn*, for example, can challenge even the most determined reader. Other books, such as Geoffrey Chaucer's (1992/1472) *Canterbury Tales,* may use forms of English appropriate to the time and place in which they were written but unfamiliar to 21st century students.

Knowledge Demands

The last dimension of qualitative evaluation is the knowledge demands a text poses. Book content ranges from familiar, mundane experiences about everyday events that all students have encountered to texts that explore unfamiliar circumstances or topics that require historical or literary background knowledge. One challenge of reading *Canterbury Tales*, for example, is clearly the language, but also the understanding of the social customs, cultural conventions, and attitudes in terms of religion, class differences, and other aspects of English life at the time. For some texts, students need to know a lot about a specific topic like science, or about particular geographical regions, while other texts require little or no background knowledge of this sort. Take *Find the Constellations* (Rey, 1954), for instance. The author shares information about stars, including "sky-views" of constellations as seen from different places on earth. It might be helpful for students to understand how the latitude of a person observing the sky affects the relative positions of the stars as they form patterns called *constellations*. In addition, levels of knowledge about particular cultures can impact student understanding when reading texts outside their own cultural experiences. For example, *Homeless Bird* (Whelan, 2000), a story about an Indian girl who is widowed as a child bride, might pose challenges for students unfamiliar with marriage customs in India, which once regularly included arranged marriages among children.

Tools for Assessing Text Complexity

The qualitative text complexity rubrics in figures 2.1 and 2.2 (pages 27–34), for both narrative and informational texts, provide templates for thinking about text complexity in relation to your students. These rubrics identify the qualitative features that should be considered when evaluating a narrative or informational text, respectively, to determine its complexity. Using these, a teacher can score a text on multiple features to determine if it is (1) an easy or comfortable text, (2) a moderate or grade-level text, or (3) a challenging or stretch text. It is these areas of potential challenge that will become the teaching points for close reading lessons.

	Consideration	1 Easy or Comfortable Text	2 Moderate or Grade-Level Text	3 Challenging or Stretch Text
Dimension 1: Understanding the General Meaning of the Text	Main Ideas	The text contains simple ideas with one level of meaning conveyed through obvious literary devices.	The text contains some complex ideas with more than one level of meaning conveyed through subtle literary devices.	The text includes substantial ideas with several levels of inferred meaning conveyed through highly sophisticated literary devices.
	Key Details	Key details support the story theme and character development.	Key details weakly support the story theme and character development.	Key details that should support the story theme or character development are not apparent; much is left to the interpretation of the reader.
Dimension 2: Understanding the Workings of the Text— Structure, Craft, Vocabulary	Organization	The text follows a simple, conventional, chronological plot pattern with few or no shifts in point of view or time; plot is highly predictable.	The text organization is somewhat unconventional; may have two or more story lines and some shifts in time and point of view; plot is sometimes hard to predict.	The text organization is intricate and unconventional, with multiple subplots and shifts in time and point of view; plot is unpredictable.

Figure 2.1: Qualitative scoring rubric for narrative text.   CONTINUED →

	Consideration	**1** **Easy or Comfortable Text**	**2** **Moderate or Grade-Level Text**	**3** **Challenging or Stretch Text**
Dimension 2: Understanding the Workings of the Text— Structure, Craft, Vocabulary	Visual Supports and Layout	Text placement is consistent throughout the text and includes a large readable font. Illustrations directly support text content.	Text placement may include columns, text interrupted by illustrations, or other variations; uses a smaller font size. Illustrations support the text directly but may include images that require synthesis of text.	Text placement includes columns and many inconsistencies as well as very small font size. Few illustrations that support the text directly; most require deep analysis and synthesis.
	Relationships Among Ideas	Relationships among ideas or characters are clear and obvious.	Relationships among ideas or characters are subtle and complex.	Relationships among ideas or characters are complex, embedded, and must be inferred.
	Vocabulary	Vocabulary is accessible, familiar, and can be determined through context clues.	Vocabulary combines familiar terms with academic vocabulary appropriate to the grade level.	Vocabulary includes extensive academic vocabulary, including many unfamiliar terms.
	Author's Purpose	The purpose of the text is simple, clear, concrete, and easy to identify.	The purpose of the text is somewhat subtle, requires interpretation, or is abstract.	The purpose of the text is abstract, implicit, may be ambiguous, and is revealed through the totality of the text.

	Consideration	1 **Easy or Comfortable Text**	2 **Moderate or Grade-Level Text**	3 **Challenging or Stretch Text**
Dimension 3: Understanding the Deep Meaning of the Text— Language and Its Use	Author's Style and Tone	The style of the text is explicit and easy to comprehend, and the tone is conversational.	The style of the text combines explicit with complex meanings, and the tone is somewhat formal.	The style of the text is abstract, and the language is ambiguous and generally unfamiliar. The tone may be somewhat unfamiliar to readers, such as an ironic tone.
	Theme	The theme or message of the text is stated explicitly by the author.	The theme or message of the text may not be stated directly, but can be easily inferred by the reader.	The theme or message of the text is not stated directly by the author and must be inferred through careful reading of the text.
	Point of View	The story is told from a single point of view (first, second, or third person) throughout.	The story is told from more than one point of view, and may incorporate multiple characters' points of view that are easily identified by the reader.	The story is told from multiple points of view, including the viewpoints of different characters that are not always easily identified by the reader.

CONTINUED →

	Consideration	1 Easy or Comfortable Text	2 Moderate or Grade-Level Text	3 Challenging or Stretch Text
Dimension 3: Understanding the Deep Meaning of the Text— Language and Its Use	Use of Language	The author uses a limited amount of symbolism or figurative language; language is explicit and can be interpreted literally.	The author conveys the meaning through some use of figurative language, including imagery, metaphor, symbolism, simile, and personification, but also includes examples and explanations that support interpreting the meaning.	The author conveys the meaning through extensive use of figurative language and provides very limited explanations or examples.
	Language Register	The text is written using a language register or form that is familiar to the reader (as opposed to an unfamiliar form like Old English, extensive use of dialect, and so on).	The text is written using a language register or form that contains some language conventions and vernacular that are not familiar to the reader.	The text is written using a language register or form that includes extensive variations of standard English that are unfamiliar to the reader.

	Consideration	1 Easy or Comfortable Text	2 Moderate or Grade-Level Text	3 Challenging or Stretch Text
Dimension 4: Meeting Knowledge Demands	Background Knowledge	The content addresses familiar cultural and historical knowledge and portrays common life experiences; everyday cultural or literary knowledge is required.	The content addresses some cultural knowledge that may not be familiar and portrays experiences that are both common and less common; some cultural, historical, or literary background knowledge is required.	The content includes heavy references to cultural or historical knowledge that is not readily familiar to those from other cultures and portrays experiences that are unfamiliar to most readers; extensive depth of cultural, historical, or literary background knowledge is required.

Source: Adapted from Lapp, Moss, Grant, & Johnson, 2015. Used with permission.

	Consideration	1 Easy or Comfortable Text	2 Moderate or Grade-Level Text	3 Challenging or Stretch Text
Dimension 1: Understanding the General Meaning of the Text	Main Ideas	Ideas are clear, obvious, and explicitly stated.	Ideas are somewhat complex; some are explicitly stated, but some require inference.	Ideas are highly abstract and most must be inferred.
	Key Details	Key details are explicitly stated.	Some details are explicitly stated, but some require inference.	Most details must be inferred.

Figure 2.2: Qualitative scoring rubric for informational text.

CONTINUED →

	Consideration	1 Easy or Comfortable Text	2 Moderate or Grade-Level Text	3 Challenging or Stretch Text
Dimension 2: Understanding the Workings of the Text— Structure, Craft, Vocabulary	Organization	There is a single, clear text structure.	Text features multiple structures; may be discipline specific, with a single thesis.	Text is intricate, with multiple structures, multiple theses, and sophisticated organization.
	Visual Supports and Layout	Text placement is consistent with readable font, simple charts, tables, and so on, with easy-to-understand headings.	Text placement includes columns; medium font size; text interrupted with visuals, complex charts, tables, and so on; and headings and subheadings requiring interpretation.	Text placement is inconsistent and features small font size, with intricate charts, tables, and so on, and headings and subheadings requiring inference and synthesis.
	Relationships Among Ideas	Relationships among ideas or characters are clear and explicitly stated.	Relationships among ideas or characters are implicit or subtle.	Relationships among ideas or characters are intricate, deep, and subtle.
	Vocabulary	Text includes some subject-specific vocabulary, with many familiar terms supported by context clues.	Text includes subject-specific vocabulary, with many unfamiliar terms with limited support from context clues.	Text includes highly academic, subject-specific, demanding vocabulary that is context dependent.
	Author's Purpose	The purpose is simple, clear, concrete, and obvious.	The purpose is subtle or abstract; requires interpretation.	The purpose is very abstract; must be inferred.

	Consideration	**1** **Easy or Comfortable Text**	**2** **Moderate or Grade-Level Text**	**3** **Challenging or Stretch Text**
Dimension 3: Understanding the Deep Meaning of the Text— Language and Its Use	Author's Style and Tone	Style is conversational, with narrative elements.	Style is objective, with passive constructions, compound sentences, and a formal tone.	Style is specific to a discipline, with dense concepts and complex sentences with an extremely formal tone.
	Theme	The theme is obvious and clearly stated.	The theme is not obvious but is easily inferred.	The theme requires inference based on careful reading.
	Point of View	The point of view is clearly stated in the text.	The point of view is easily inferred by the reader.	The point of view requires careful reading to infer.
	Uses of Language	Text contains common, explicitly disciplinary language that can be interpreted literally.	Text includes less familiar disciplinary language, with explanations that support interpretation of meaning.	Text is highly sophisticated disciplinary language that does not include supports for interpretation.
	Language Register	Text uses familiar language register or form (as opposed to an unfamiliar form like Old English, extensive use of dialect, and so on).	Text uses language register or form with some unfamiliar language conventions or vernacular.	Text uses unfamiliar language register or form, which includes extensive variations of standard English.

CONTINUED →

	Consideration	1 Easy or Comfortable Text	2 Moderate or Grade-Level Text	3 Challenging or Stretch Text
Dimension 4: Meeting Knowledge	Background Knowledge	Content addresses common, familiar cultural and historical knowledge and information familiar to students.	Content requires some background knowledge that may be unfamiliar to students and references some unfamiliar cultural knowledge.	Content includes heavy references to cultural or historical knowledge that may be unfamiliar to those from other cultures and is highly technical, requiring deep background knowledge about specific information.

Source: Adapted from Lapp, Moss, Grant, & Johnson, 2015. Used with permission.

The following sample annotated rubrics illustrate the kind of thinking teachers do as they analyze texts for complexity. Figure 2.3 features an annotated rubric for the narrative text *Tacky the Penguin* (Lester, 1988). Kindergarten teacher Karen Mallory added her notes to the rubric as she prepared to teach her students to read this narrative text. Many aspects of the text should not pose difficulty for her students; the key details are easily identified, the text structure is clear and obvious, the purpose is evident, the tone is conversational, and the theme and point of view are easy to grasp. Potential areas of challenge for young readers include the layout, vocabulary, relationships among ideas (in this case, among characters), and the theme of the text, which focuses on uniqueness.

	Consideration	**1** **Easy or** **Comfortable** **Text**	**2** **Moderate or** **Grade-Level** **Text**	**3** **Challenging** **or Stretch** **Text**
Dimension 1: **Understanding** **the General** **Meaning of the** **Text**	Main Ideas	Ideas are clear, obvious, and explicitly stated.	Ideas are somewhat complex; some are explicitly stated, but some require inference. *Some students may not understand the main idea of being yourself even though you might be different. This is not explicitly stated.*	Ideas are highly abstract and most must be inferred.
	Key Details	Key details are explicitly stated. *Details are clear for students and explicitly stated (Tacky slaps the hunters on the backs, sings loudly and dreadfully).*	Some details are explicitly stated, but some require inference.	Most details must be inferred.
Dimension 2: **Understanding** **the Workings** **of the Text—** **Structure, Craft,** **Vocabulary**	Organization	There is a single, clear text structure. *The text is in sequential order with a clear structure.*	Text features multiple structures; may be discipline specific, with a single thesis.	Text is intricate, with multiple structures, multiple theses, and sophisticated organization.

Figure 2.3: Qualitative rubric for narrative text *Tacky the Penguin* (Lester, 1988) with teacher annotations.

CONTINUED →

	Consideration	**1** **Easy or Comfortable Text**	**2** **Moderate or Grade-Level Text**	**3** **Challenging or Stretch Text**
Dimension 2: Understanding the Workings of the Text— Structure, Craft, Vocabulary	Visual Supports and Layout	Text placement is consistent, with readable font, simple charts, tables, and so on with easy-to-understand headings.	Text placement includes columns; medium font size; text interrupted with visuals, complex charts, tables, and so on; and headings and subheadings requiring interpretation. *Most of the text is consistent and matches illustrations. Students might be confused by the layout when the author describes Tacky's marching as "1-2-3, 4-2, 3-6-0, 2½, 0."*	Text placement is inconsistent and features small font size, with intricate charts, tables, and so on, and headings and subheadings requiring inference and synthesis.

	Consideration	1 Easy or Comfortable Text	2 Moderate or Grade-Level Text	3 Challenging or Stretch Text
Dimension 2: Understanding the Workings of the Text— Structure, Craft, Vocabulary	Relationships Among Ideas	Relationships among ideas or characters are clear and explicitly stated.	Relationships among ideas or characters are implicit or subtle. *Students may understand the relationship between the hunters and the penguins but not understand Tacky's relationship with the other penguins.*	Relationships among ideas or characters are intricate, deep, and subtle.
	Vocabulary	Text includes some subject-specific vocabulary, with many familiar terms supported by context clues.	Text includes subject-specific vocabulary, with many unfamiliar terms with limited support from context clues. *Some words may challenge students (companions, switch, hearty slap).*	Text includes highly academic, subject-specific, demanding vocabulary that is context dependent.

CONTINUED →

	Consideration	1 Easy or Comfortable Text	2 Moderate or Grade-Level Text	3 Challenging or Stretch Text
Dimension 2: Understanding the Workings of the Text— Structure, Craft, Vocabulary	Author's Purpose	The purpose is simple, clear, concrete, and obvious. *The purpose is simple, and students would understand that they are being entertained.*	The purpose is subtle or abstract; requires interpretation.	The purpose is very abstract; must be inferred.
Dimension 3: Understanding the Deep Meaning of the Text— Language and Its Use	Author's Style and Tone	Style is conversational, with narrative elements. *The text is written in a conversational tone that students would find familiar.*	Style is objective, with passive constructions, compound sentences, and a formal tone.	Style is specific to a discipline, with dense concepts and complex sentences with an extremely formal tone.
	Theme	The theme is obvious and clearly stated.	The theme is not obvious but is easily inferred.	The theme requires inference based on careful reading. *The theme of being unique and who you are is not explicitly stated.*

	Consideration	**1** **Easy or Comfortable Text**	**2** **Moderate or Grade-Level Text**	**3** **Challenging or Stretch Text**
Dimension 3: Understanding the Deep Meaning of the Text— Language and Its Use	Point of View	The point of view is clearly stated in the text.	The point of view is easily inferred by the reader. *Although not always explicitly stated, the quotation marks and illustrations help students know the third person point of view.*	The point of view requires careful reading to infer.
	Uses of Language	Text contains common, explicitly disciplinary language that can be interpreted literally. *The common use of language will not confuse students.*	Text is includes less familiar disciplinary language, with explanations that support interpretation of meaning.	Text is highly sophisticated disciplinary language that does not include supports for interpretation.
	Language Register	Text uses familiar language register or form (as opposed to an unfamiliar form like Old English, extensive use of dialect, and so on). *Familiar language is used throughout the text.*	Text uses language register or form with some unfamiliar language conventions or vernacular.	Text uses unfamiliar language register or form, which includes extensive variations of standard English.

CONTINUED →

	Consideration	1 Easy or Comfortable Text	2 Moderate or Grade-Level Text	3 Challenging or Stretch Text
Dimension 4: Meeting Knowledge	Background Knowledge	Content addresses common, familiar cultural and historical knowledge and information familiar to students.	Content requires some background knowledge that may be unfamiliar to students and references some unfamiliar cultural knowledge. *Students may be unfamiliar with why penguins are hunted animals.*	Content includes heavy references to cultural or historical knowledge that may be unfamiliar to those from other cultures and is highly technical, requiring deep background knowledge about specific information.

Source: Adapted from Lapp, Moss, Grant, & Johnson, 2015. Used with permission.

Figure 2.4 features an annotated rubric for an informational text, *Eye to Eye: How Animals See the World* (Jenkins, 2014). Third-grade teacher Debbie Sol added her notes to the rubric as she prepared to teach her students to read this informational text. As even a cursory glance at the rubric indicates, she has evaluated this text as being at or above grade level in most areas. Her notes reveal the target areas she will address in her instruction.

	Consideration	1 Easy or Comfortable Text	2 Moderate or Grade-Level Text	3 Challenging or Stretch Text
Dimension 1: Understanding the General Meaning of the Text	Main Ideas	Ideas are clear, obvious, and explicitly stated.	Ideas are somewhat complex; some are explicitly stated, but some require inference.	Ideas are highly abstract and most must be inferred. *Students must understand foundational concepts about structure of eyes and the role of light in seeing.*

	Consideration	1 Easy or Comfortable Text	2 Moderate or Grade-Level Text	3 Challenging or Stretch Text
Dimension 1: Understanding the General Meaning of the Text	Key Details	Key details are explicitly stated.	Some details are explicitly stated, but some require inference. *In some places the text is very straightforward, but there are sections where meaning is inferred or implied. For example, the author writes, "The snail's eyes can resolve images, but they function mainly as light detectors." Students need to infer that "resolve images" means the snails can see objects, and they need to know that light is needed for vision.*	Most details must be inferred.

Figure 2.4: Qualitative rubric for informational text *Eye to Eye: How Animals See the World* (Jenkins, 2014) with teacher annotations.

CONTINUED →

	Consideration	1 Easy or Comfortable Text	2 Moderate or Grade-Level Text	3 Challenging or Stretch Text
Dimension 2: Understanding the Workings of the Text— Structure, Craft, Vocabulary	Organization	There is a single, clear text structure.	Text features multiple structures; may be discipline specific, with a single thesis. *Bold print and headings are clear and helpful.*	Text is intricate, with multiple structures, multiple theses, and sophisticated organization.
	Visual Supports and Layout	Text placement is consistent, with readable font, simple charts, tables, and so on, with easy-to-understand headings.	Text placement includes columns; medium font size; text interrupted with visuals, complex charts, tables, and so on; and headings and subheadings requiring interpretation. *Illustrations focus on animal type being discussed.*	Text placement is Inconsistent, and features small font size, with intricate charts, tables, and so on, and headings and subheadings requiring inference and synthesis.
	Relationships Among Ideas	Relationships among ideas or characters are clear and explicitly stated.	Relationships among ideas or characters are implicit or subtle. *Relationships are clear—eyes are discussed for each organism presented. The pattern is logical.*	Relationships among ideas or characters are intricate, deep, and subtle.

	Consideration	1 Easy or Comfortable Text	2 Moderate or Grade-Level Text	3 Challenging or Stretch Text
Dimension 2: Understanding the Workings of the Text— Structure, Craft, Vocabulary	Vocabulary	Text includes some subject-specific vocabulary, with many familiar terms supported by context clues.	Text includes subject-specific vocabulary, with many unfamiliar terms with limited support from context clues.	Text includes highly academic, subject-specific, demanding vocabulary that is context dependent. *The text contains specific science terms and academic language that will be unfamiliar to most students: perceive, discern, sensing, and so on.*
	Author's Purpose	The purpose is simple, clear, concrete, and obvious.	The purpose is subtle or abstract; requires interpretation. *Students will understand, after reading several pages, that this book is informing them about the variations in eyes among different animals.*	The purpose is very abstract; must be inferred.

CONTINUED →

	Consideration	1 Easy or Comfortable Text	2 Moderate or Grade-Level Text	3 Challenging or Stretch Text
Dimension 3: Understanding the Deep Meaning of the Text— Language and Its Use	Author's Style and Tone	Style is conversational, with narrative elements.	Style is objective, with passive constructions, compound sentences, and a formal tone. *The writing style is formal but approachable. Students have worked with texts with a similar tone.*	Style is specific to a discipline, with dense concepts and complex sentences with an extremely formal tone.
	Theme	The theme is obvious and clearly stated.	The theme is not obvious but is easily inferred. *Again, after reading a few pages, students might infer that different animals have different eyes, suitable for varying habitats and ways of life.*	The theme requires inference based on careful reading.
	Point of View	The point of view is clearly stated in the text.	The point of view is easily inferred by the reader. *The text is informational, from a narrator's perspective.*	The point of view requires careful reading to infer.

	Consideration	1 Easy or Comfortable Text	2 Moderate or Grade-Level Text	3 Challenging or Stretch Text
Dimension 3: Understanding the Deep Meaning of the Text— Language and Its Use	Uses of Language	Text contains common, explicitly disciplinary language that can be interpreted literally.	Text includes less familiar disciplinary language, with explanations that support interpretation of meaning.	Text is highly sophisticated disciplinary language that does not include supports for interpretation. *The text is full of discipline-specific language that might be hard to discern. Retina, compound lenses, and arthropods are a few examples.*
	Language Register	Text uses familiar language register or form (as opposed to an unfamiliar form like Old English, extensive use of dialect, and so on).	Text uses language register or form with some unfamiliar language conventions or vernacular. *The text uses a familiar science register, but it is somewhat sophisticated for third graders.*	Text uses unfamiliar language register or form, which includes extensive variations of standard English.

CONTINUED →

	Consideration	1 Easy or Comfortable Text	2 Moderate or Grade-Level Text	3 Challenging or Stretch Text
Dimension 4: Meeting Knowledge	Background Knowledge	Content addresses common, familiar cultural and historical knowledge and information familiar to students.	Content requires some background knowledge that may be unfamiliar to students and references some unfamiliar cultural knowledge.	Content includes heavy references to cultural or historical knowledge that may be unfamiliar to those from other cultures and is highly technical, requiring deep background knowledge about specific information. *This is a technical text for these students; it seems to require some understanding of eye function and the role of light in seeing.*

Source: Adapted from Lapp, Moss, Grant, & Johnson, 2015. Used with permission.

Reader and Task Factors

As we think about readers and tasks, we consider our students in relation to the texts they will read and the tasks they will complete in response to those texts. After all, we can't consider texts or tasks in isolation from our students. Student needs come sharply into focus with close reading, since many students aren't used to reading and rereading to dig deeply into a text, and instead read for surface information in a cursory way.

Reading and cognitive skills, prior knowledge and experience, motivation and engagement, and specific task concerns are all critical aspects of the reader and task equation (see figure 2.5). The questions provided in figure 2.5 can guide teachers as they consider the challenges their students will face when encountering a new complex text. In addition to identifying the potential challenges, the "next steps" questions prompt teachers to consider how they will support students as they address those challenges during close reading.

Reading and Cognitive Skills			
	Yes	**No**	**Comments**
Do my students have the literal- and critical-comprehension skills to understand this text? If not, how will I scaffold the information?			
Will this text promote the development of critical-thinking skills in my students?			
What are my next instructional steps to support my students having a context for successfully reading the selected text?			
Prior Knowledge and Experience			
	Yes	**No**	**Comments**
Will my students grasp the purpose for reading the text?			
Do my students have the prior knowledge required for navigating this text?			
Do my students have the academic vocabulary required for navigating this text?			
Are my students familiar with this particular genre and its characteristics?			
Do my students have the maturity level required to address the text content?			
What are my next instructional steps to support my students having a context for successfully reading the selected text?			
Motivation and Engagement			
	Yes	**No**	**Comments**
Will my students be motivated to read this text based on its content?			
Will my students be motivated to read this text based on its writing style?			
Do my students have the reading stamina to stick with this text with my support?			
What are my next instructional steps to support my students having a context for successfully reading the selected text?			

Figure 2.5: Reader and task checklist.

CONTINUED →

Specific Task Concerns			
	Yes	No	Comments
Do my students have experience with this type of task?			
Is the task appropriate for my students? (For example, have I created a moderately difficult task if the text is very challenging, created a more challenging task for an easier text, or both?)			
What are my next instructional steps to support my students having a context for successfully reading the selected text?			

Source: Adapted from Lapp, Moss, Grant, & Johnson, 2015. Used with permission.
Visit **go.SolutionTree.com/literacy** for a free reproducible version of this figure.

While we, as teachers, have given much attention to reading and cognitive skills and prior knowledge and experience, far less attention has been given to issues of motivation and engagement and specific task concerns. For example, teachers need to consider student motivation and interest when selecting texts, since research clearly indicates that greater reader engagement results in stronger comprehension (Guthrie & Cox, 2001). Language and literacy development expert Catherine Snow (2013) argues that a *collapse of motivation* occurs when the selected text is too hard, too long, too full of unknown words, or about an unknown topic, and the reader

> quickly exhausts his or her initial willingness to struggle with it. . . . The reality of reading a text that is too hard without any help is that it often results, not in productive struggle, but in destructive frustration." (p. 19)

Therefore, if teachers pick texts that are not only complex but also motivating and engaging, the likelihood of student success may be increased.

In addition, it is imperative that we give attention to the nature of the task we assign in response to a particular text. Experts have given little attention to the types of tasks we assign students during close reading (Hiebert & Pearson, 2014). It is important that teachers carefully design the performance tasks they want students to complete in response to close readings, maintaining an optimum balance between text and task. Researchers Karen Wixson and Sheila Valencia (2014) state that text complexity is more than just qualitative and quantitative features of the text but also a function of the interaction among reader, text, and task factors in a specific situation. They argue that teachers can identify tasks in relation to specific texts that accommodate students at a range of abilities and provide instruction that addresses these differences. The 2010 National Teacher of the Year Sarah Brown Wessling (n.d.) argues that the more challenging the outcome task, the more accessible the text should be to readers. When she introduces students to literary theory, for example, which demands a challenging outcome task, she uses far more accessible texts than when introducing more familiar concepts. According to Valencia (n.d.):

> We must never think about text complexity in isolation from the
> reading task, the reader, and the context. Exhorting students to
> try harder or to read more closely as they encounter the new,
> more challenging texts is unlikely to improve comprehension.
> (p. 27)

A further consideration involves reflecting on the tasks we assign in connection with the type of complex text to be studied. The tasks assigned must be appropriate to the genre being studied. For example, with expository text, students will not typically be involved in the identification of literary devices like metaphors, similes, alliteration, and so on, since these features are not typically found in exposition. They are, however, often found in fiction and in literary nonfiction, which combines features of both fiction and nonfiction.

Conclusion

The close reading of complex texts is crucial to meeting standards and making sure students are college and career ready. Effective text-complexity evaluation relies equally on all three factors: quantitative features, qualitative features, and reader and task factors; teachers must consider each when selecting a text that is complex enough for students to read closely. Neglecting any of these factors when determining text complexity can result in problems. For instance, just picking books based on Lexile measures may provide a complex text but will give you no real information on the challenging areas in a book. Omitting consideration of reader and task factors can be equally problematic because the selected text will not be related to your students' strengths and instructional needs. The tools we've provided in this chapter will enable you to take all of these factors into consideration when evaluating complex texts to use as part of a lesson.

3 Making Decisions That Support Close Reading Instruction

Now that we've defined close reading, and identified the factors that make a text complex, let's briefly consider some key decisions that you must address as you prepare a lesson to support your students in becoming close readers of increasingly complex texts. You make the following decisions as a result of your assessments of student performance. It's important to remember that the decisions teachers make greatly affect student learning (Vescio, Ross, & Adams, 2008). These decisions can also help you assess your own progress as a teacher of close reading; as you gain experience with the process, your decisions about what constitutes a complex text become more obvious, the questions that support students being able to analyze these areas of complexity will be easier to craft, and the scaffolds that you design to support all students becoming close readers will become more differentiated.

Decision 1: Identify Your Lesson Purpose

Because there is so much emphasis on teaching students to closely read short, complex texts, there's a temptation to just select any short passage, even though it may not be related to the lesson purpose, to engage students in a close reading. Doing this would be the opposite of what should occur. Once you identify your lesson purpose that is, of course, related to the standards being addressed, you can then select a text and plan a close reading as one dimension of the instruction designed to accomplish the purpose. While we list possible texts to support sample lesson purposes, it's important to note that the text should be selected *after* the lesson purpose has been identified because the study of the text should help accomplish the purpose. We mention these texts here merely as examples of the relationship that should exist between a content purpose statement and a text selected to help students achieve the purpose. Also note that while we identify texts that are related to the accomplishment of a specific lesson purpose, we are not suggesting that an entire book be used for a close reading. A text or passage selected for close reading should be short—approximately one page—because students will be reading it more than once.

- **Grades K–1 science lesson purpose:** Identify the sequence involved in a seed becoming a plant. A perfect text to support accomplishing this lesson purpose is Clyde Robert Bulla's (2001) *A Tree Is a Plant*. This text can also be found in appendix B of the Common Core Standards (NGA & CCSSO, n.d.b).

- **Grades 3–5 literature and social studies lesson purpose:** Realize differences exist among people. This is a topic that is often addressed with various titles across the intermediate grades. Texts that would work well for close reading include

  - Adler, D. A. (2003). *Mama played baseball*. San Diego, CA: Gulliver Books.

  - Ellis, D. (2001). *The breadwinner*. Berkeley, CA: Publishers Group West.

  - Little, J. (1989). About feeling Jewish. In *Hey world, here I am!* (pp. 52–53). New York: Harper & Row.

  - Swain, G. (2012). Margaret Batchelder, immigrant inspector. In *Hope and tears: Ellis Island voices* (pp. 46–47). Honesdale, PA: Calkins Creek.

- **Middle school science lesson purpose:** Explore the moon, planets, asteroids, comets, or other objects in outer space. Using a subsection of a chapter on planets would be an appropriate text. An additional text that would work well is "Space Probe" in *Astronomy and Space: From the Big Bang to the Big Crunch* (Engelbert, 2009). This excerpt appears in appendix B of the CCSS (NGA & CCSSO, n.d.).

- **High school US history lesson purpose:** Understand the complexities of the phrase "freedom for all." Possible text for this lesson includes Earl Warren's decision (National Museum of American History, n.d.) delivered in the case of *Brown v. Board of Education of Topeka* (1954). Another text that supports this purpose and works well for a close reading is the primary source document the Civil Rights Act of 1964, which was signed into law by Lyndon Johnson (http://media.nara.gov/rediscovery/02233_2011_001_a.jpg). See appendix D of *Teaching Tolerance* (2015) for additional texts.

As these examples suggest, there are numerous texts or text segments that can be closely read with the goal being to support accomplishing a well-defined lesson purpose.

Decision 2: Select the Text

Once the standards and lesson purpose have been identified, teachers can select appropriately complex texts that support accomplishing the purpose. The text selected for a close reading should be one that contains language, information, and structural features that are worth pondering. Lots of texts that students read have a very straightforward story line, information, or vocabulary that is easily understood. These are not the ones to use for a close reading. The text selected for close reading should contain thought-provoking language, ideas, and information that one must reread and think and talk about in order to truly comprehend the text's deeper meaning. It should be short and yet complete enough to encourage students to think deeply about its content. It could be a complete poem, section from a science text, mathematics problem, or historical letter. The important feature is that it contains enough depth of information to be worthy of reading several times. As the reader does so, he or she should find the text challenging. Close reading experiences usually involve reading short, engaging texts, and these reading experiences can often lead to students independently reading the entire book.

Through well-chosen excerpts, teachers can ignite student interest and excitement for a variety of topics that will lead them to independent reading experiences in areas of deep interest. Rather than an unpleasant chore, close reading experiences can be a catalyst for further reading.

As we mentioned in chapter 2, the Common Core State Standards (NGA & CCSSO, 2010) suggest that educators should determine complexity by evaluating three factors. The first is the text's quantitative or countable features, such as number of words in a sentence and number of syllables in a word. The second is the text's qualitative features, such as familiarity with the language and meaning. The third and most significant factor is who is reading the text and what task the reader is being asked to do. This third factor makes it quite clear that the degree of complexity can increase or decrease based on the reader's knowledge of the topic, the language, the structure or type of text, the student's reading skills, and the tasks the reader is expected to perform. The more background knowledge a reader has about a topic, the less complex the passage becomes.

Decision 3: Create Text-Dependent Questions

The questions that teachers create should cause the reader to think about what the text says, how the text works, and what the text means. After teachers have selected a text, they should anticipate student difficulties and plan possible questions and prompts they might pose to encourage students' close reading, analysis, and understanding of the text. You may often begin by asking questions that support students in gaining a general understanding of what the text says. As a way to examine the text's big idea, you might ask questions that cause students to consider the who, what, where, when, why, and how of the information. When asking questions that invite readers to consider key details, be sure students are developing the general understanding of the text rather than bogging themselves down with bits of information that don't enable them to see the major ideas. The questions you ask should cause the reader to scrutinize the text for the answer. Pay careful attention to determine if the focus is on what the text says, how it works, and what it means.

Remember that you do not have to ask the questions you plan in a linear fashion, and you do not have to ask all of them. They are your guide. By listening to your students' responses and viewing their annotations, you will know what questions you need to ask to push their thinking and understanding. For close reading, it is essential that teachers use text-dependent questions, rather than text-independent ones. The focus of the question should draw students' attention to a specific area of complexity the teacher feels they may be wrestling with. For example, if the teacher has determined that the language of the text might be the area of complexity that would interfere with the students' understanding of the text, the questions asked should focus the students on analyzing the language. This would also be true for areas such as structure, author purpose, and so on. In the examples we provide later in this chapter in tables 3.2–3.4 (pages 57–60), notice that the questions being asked have been strategically designed to support students' comprehension of a particular area that has been identified as complex for this group of students. As a general rule, text-dependent questions are preferable to text-independent questions, but there may occasionally be times during shared, guided, or independent reading when you ask text-independent questions. However, it is not necessary to ask questions that do not support a deepening of the students' understanding.

The text-dependent questions teachers ask strategically should take students on a journey through the text that begins with developing their general or literal, but significant, understanding of the information or story line. This occurs as students are directed through questions that cause them to consider central themes, key ideas and details, and the development of characters or ideas. Paying close attention to the types of questions students are answering easily and those that cause them to struggle provides insights regarding how well they understand the text. If some students are unable to draw reasonable conclusions about the text information at the end of a close reading, they probably need additional time to further explore the text with the teacher.

Deeper understanding occurs as students consider the text's mechanics or workings. Questions should cause them to consider the selected vocabulary, how the text is organized or structured, and the craft or techniques the author uses to share information. This includes looking at the language to determine if the author uses devices like simile, metaphor, and irony or parallel structures, short sentences, or long structurally complex sentences. Students consider how these choices affect tone, indicate the author's point of view or purpose, and affect the presentation of information. As understanding deepens, next questions should cause readers to dig even deeper to analyze and infer intent, arguments, and claims. Each question you ask should require the reader to return to the text to support interpretation.

Table 3.1 illustrates the difference between text-independent and text-dependent questions for *The 13 Clocks* (Thurber, 1950) and identifies the different focus of each question. We provide the text excerpt in question from Thurber (1950) here to facilitate your understanding of how the different types of questions apply in this example:

> Once upon a time, in a gloomy castle on a lonely hill, where there were thirteen clocks that wouldn't go, there lived a cold aggressive Duke, and his niece, the Princess Saralinda. She was warm in every wind and weather, but he was always cold. His hands were as cold as his smile and almost as cold as his heart. He wore gloves when he was asleep, and he wore gloves when he was awake, which made it difficult for him to pick up pins or coins or kernels of nuts, or to tear the wings from nightingales. He was six feet four, and forty-six, and even colder than

he thought he was. One eye wore a velvet patch; the other glittered through a monocle, which made half of his body seem closer to you than the other half. He had lost one eye when he was twelve, for he was fond of peering into nests and lairs in search of birds and animals to maul. One afternoon, a mother shrike had mauled him first. His nights were spent in evil dreams, and his days were given to wicked schemes.

Wickedly scheming, he would limp and cackle through the cold corridors of the castle, planning new impossible feats for the suitors of Saralinda to perform. He did not wish to give her hand in marriage, since her hand was the only warm hand in the castle. Even the hands of his watch and the hands of all the thirteen clocks were frozen. They had all frozen at the same time, on a snowy night, seven years before, and after that it was always ten to five in the castle. Travelers and mariners would look up at the gloomy castle on the lonely hill and say, "Time lies frozen there. It's always Then. It's never Now." (Thurber, 1950, as cited in NGA & CCSSO, n.d.b, p. 46)

Table 3.1: Differences Between Text-Independent and Text-Dependent Questions

Text-Independent Question	Focus of Text-Independent Question	Text-Dependent Question	Focus of Text-Dependent Question
What kinds of stories are set in castles?	Reader's opinion	What is the setting of the text?	What the text says
Describe a person you know who is cold and evil.	Reader's experience	How does the phrase "His nights were spent in evil dreams, and his days were given to wicked schemes" help you understand the Duke's character (NGA & CCSSO, n.d.b, p. 46)?	How the text works
What kinds of things might someone have to do to prove they are worthy of marrying a princess?	Reader's experience	What is likely to be the fate of the princess? What text evidence supports your ideas?	What the text means

When creating questions, teachers will benefit from considering two important factors: (1) depth of knowledge and (2) significance of questions.

Depth of Knowledge

Questions should systematically move students across Webb's Depth of Knowledge (DOK) model (Webb, 1997, 1999; Webb et al., 2005, 2006), a four-level system for categorizing tasks based on the complexity of completing them. Level 1 involves the recall and recognition of information that is stated literally. Level 2 involves using skills to identify, summarize, solve, and describe information. Level 3 calls for strategic thinking that includes formulating, hypothesizing, citing evidence, and drawing conclusions, and level 4 includes comparing and contrasting information, critiquing author intent, and constructing arguments. At level 4, readers are being engaged in tasks that move them well beyond a general level of comprehension. They are not just consumers of information but rather, at this stage of knowing, they are able to use information and insights they have gained to craft new information. In order for comprehension to grow, readers must be able to describe, explain, and interpret information as they develop each level of understanding. Questions should move students through text analysis as they gain a general understanding and recognize how the text works and what it means. Referring to this system when planning instruction helps to ensure that tasks being designed increase in complexity.

Let's explore questions about a text and its structure and meaning as related to Webb's levels using Susan B. Anthony's (1873) speech, "Women's Right to Suffrage" (available at www.nationalcenter.org/AnthonySuffrage.html), which she delivered after she was arrested and fined $100 for voting in the 1872 presidential election. Remember that women did not have the right to vote until the passing of the Nineteenth Amendment in 1920. Notice that the questions cause the reader to think about what the text—in this case a speech—says, how it works, and what it means.

What Does the Text Say?

To build a foundation of student understanding, it is important to ask lower level (1 and 2) DOK questions to ensure that students grasp the main ideas and details of the text, which they can use as a foundation for deeper analysis. The following examples in table 3.2 are questions to help assess whether students have acquired a general understanding of this famous speech. You will probably not need to ask more than one, but listening to your students' responses and partner talk lets you know if asking additional questions is warranted. You may need to share with your students that the Constitution is the legal document that governs the United States because it is not easy to determine from this speech, and it is essential to understanding the significance of her act of voting illegally.

While being able to answer these questions certainly would suggest that readers have a general understanding, there is much more to infer about this speech's significance.

Table 3.2: What the Text Says–General Understanding and Key Detail Questions

Question	Type	DOK Level
If someone asked you what this text is about, what would you say?	General understanding	Level 1: Recall–Identify main claim
What seems to be the big idea Susan B. Anthony is sharing in this speech?	General understanding	Level 1: Recall–Identify main claim
What was Susan B. Anthony trying to accomplish?	General understanding	Level 1: Recall–Identify main claim
What caused Susan B. Anthony to be arrested?	Key detail	Level 2: Link main idea and details
What is the federal Constitution of the United States?	Key detail	Level 2: Link main ideas and details

How Does the Text Work?

Questions that cause the reader to think about how a text works push them to return to the text for deeper analysis. Again, not all questions you create will need to be asked. You will often prepare more questions than you will ask. Your determination of which and how many questions you ask should be based on the responses your students provide. (See table 3.3, page 58.) Because students must employ more sophisticated thinking and do more synthesis work when responding to these questions, we have included extended explanations and examples in the DOK Level column to clarify for readers specifically what should be happening as teachers pose questions and students respond to them by employing skills at various DOK levels. These examples are just one possible way students and teachers may approach a text.

Since there are many words in this text that students cannot define from context, you might ask students to identify all the words that are not familiar to them and then define the words during partner talk. You need to be careful that your close reading lessons do not turn into vocabulary lessons. If no context exists for determining word meanings, you may need to front-load some words. You may decide to first give students an opportunity to analyze unknown words for meaning and then, if they cannot do so, define words that are essential to the text's meaning.

Table 3.3: How the Text Works—Structure, Vocabulary, and Craft Questions

Question	Type	DOK Level
Look at paragraph 1: What does the word *alleged* mean?	Vocabulary	Level 2: Skill or concept (Students will use context to identify the meaning of the word.)
Look at paragraph 1: What does the word *indictment* mean?	Vocabulary	Level 2: Skill or concept (Students will use context to identify the meaning of the word.)
Look at the word *alleged* in paragraph 1, sentence 2: Does she believe she committed a crime?	Structure and craft	Level 2: Skill or concept (Students will craft a response by linking ideas.)
Look at paragraph 1: Instead of committing a crime, what does she believe she did?	Structure	Level 3: Strategic thinking (Students will link ideas across paragraphs. For example, students will note that Anthony keeps sharing evidence throughout her speech to promote her justification for voting, citing sentence 2 in which she exercised her right as a citizen to vote.)
Look at paragraph 2: What is meant by *preamble* to the Constitution?	Vocabulary	Level 1: Recall (If this term is not known by the readers it should be front-loaded because there is no context available to support interpretation.)
What does the preamble say?	Vocabulary and structure	Level 3: Strategic thinking (Strategic thinking links ideas across paragraphs to build the impression of the persecution of women. When students note that we as a nation have these rights, the teacher may stress the word *we* and ask students to think about whom this refers to.)
Look at paragraph 4: What did Susan B. Anthony believe was her right? Can you find evidence for how she justifies this being her right?	Structure and craft	Level 3: Strategic thinking (Strategic thinking occurs as students link ideas across paragraphs that Anthony uses as a persuasive technique to craft her argument. Teachers may direct students to look again at paragraph 4 and ask them, "Why does she believe it is a mockery to talk to women about the blessings of liberty?" with the goal of having students cite the last sentence in the paragraph that notes that women do not have the liberty to vote. Students should identify evidence Anthony intersperses throughout the speech about how we all did the work and therefore all have these rights—one of which is voting.)

Question	Type	DOK Level
Look at paragraph 5: What does she believe is the supreme law of the land? Who did she believe the constitution provided liberty for? Which group of people did she believe were not provided with this liberty?	Craft	Level 3: Strategic thinking (Students employ strategic thinking about word choices Anthony used to set the tone of injustice toward women. Students may cite Anthony's assertions that making it illegal for women to vote goes against the supreme law because this was not a part of the original law; it is *ex post facto*.)
What is meant by *disfranchisement*?	Vocabulary and craft	Level 3: Strategic thinking (Thinking involves inferring word choice and combined structure used by Anthony to promote her argument.)
In paragraph 6, what does the author mean by the phrase *hateful oligarchy of sex*?	Vocabulary and structure	Level 3: Strategic thinking (She threads these powerful words throughout as a way to ensure that the reader is feeling the injustice leveled against women through her arrest.)
In paragraph 7, who are the citizens? So who can vote?	Craft	Level 3: Strategic thinking (Anthony builds argument through tone and by language selection.)

Again, you may not need to ask all the questions you have prepared. As you listen to your students' responses, you will be able to make this determination. Please note that questions highlighting a particular feature such as vocabulary or structure were not all asked at once. Your questions should follow the flow of the text.

What Does the Text Mean?

Text-dependent questions should cause the reader to infer the author's intentions. These build on the two earlier sets of questions that identified whether or not students had acquired a general or literal understanding of the text and could support this by noting key details. Your second set of questions should have prompted students to understand vocabulary, text structure, and the craft the author uses to share information or tell a story. (See table 3.4, page 60.)

Notice that these questions were very purposefully designed to move readers from having a basic literal understanding of the text to a deep understanding of Susan B. Anthony's intent. The progression of these questions provides an opportunity for the teacher to listen to students' responses as a way to check their understanding and critical analysis. These questions cause readers to identify significant information in the text and blend into a deep analysis of Anthony's argument.

Table 3.4: What the Text Means–Author Purpose Questions

Question	Type	DOK Level
Look at paragraph 8: Why does Susan B. Anthony compare the plight of women and African Americans? (To invite the reader to conclude that all people have rights–she illustrates this by drawing a comparison to the treatment of slaves who had earlier suffered injustice.)	Author's purpose	Level 4: Extended thinking (This question causes the reader to conclude that laws should not discriminate against women; they too are citizens. This exclusion of women as voters is as invalid as it was against slaves who were freed in 1862.)
What is Susan B. Anthony's hope for women? Is she optimistic that desire will be realized? (Yes, because she directs attention to the preamble, which uses the inclusive term "We," as evidence that women, who are a part of the citizenry, have equal rights.)	Author's purpose	Level 3: Strategic thinking (Thinking involves reflecting on the bias against women, who are a part of the citizenry.)

Significance of Questions

Significant questions are ones that cause the reader to continually return to the text to identify information that supports their deepening analysis. The questions the teacher asks students as they read and discuss Susan B. Anthony's speech in the preceding examples are significant because they promote thinking about the qualitative features of the text, which include its meaning and purpose, its organizational structure, the language used, and the author's intent.

To more deeply understand the concept of significant questions, let's look at table 3.5 and contrast significant and less-significant questions for familiar texts. Notice that both sets of questions cause the reader to examine the text, but the more significant questions guide readers in making deep conclusions about the text.

Once you have selected your text, remember that the significant questions you write should cause the reader to think about the intricacies of what the text says, how it works, and what it means. In constructing these questions, be mindful of the students who will be answering them. The questions you prepare should be viewed as scaffolds that cause your students to deeply analyze the selected text. The number and type of questions you ask should be based on your continuous analysis of what areas are complex for your students. This responsive teaching (Goldman & Lee, 2014) involving your continuous

Table 3.5: Significant and Less Significant Questions

Title	Less Significant	Significant	Why
Little Red-Cap (Grimm & Grimm, 1944)	What was the color of Red Cap's hood?	Who was in Grandmother's bed when Red Cap got to her cabin?	The significant question asks the reader to identify a key detail that supports inferring that the wolf did not have good intentions and had not acted positively toward Grandmother. Answering this question causes the reader to have a general understanding of the text.

The less-significant question is considered as such because while the reader did have to find this detail in the text, it is not essential to know in order to understand the intentions of the wolf. |
| "Melting Pot" (Quindlen, 1988) | What was the author's nationality? | Why is the following sentence reflective of the author's interpretation of a melting pot? "About a third of the people in the neighborhood think of squid as calamari, about a third think of it as sushi, and about a third think of it as bait" (p. 257). | The significant question causes the reader to consider the author's craft, which is to make a comparison regarding how the different members of the neighborhood viewed the same food through the eyes of their cultures. The intent was to illustrate that while they shared the same nation, they did so through different cultural eyes. The less significant question causes the reader to access a key detail that really is not pertinent to understanding the intricacies of a US melting pot. |
| "Mini Laser for Real-Time Quality Control" (Fraunhofer-Gesellschaft, 2015) | What is the size of the laser used in this research? | Why does the author clarify that the process of chemical reactions could soon be continuously monitored in real time? | This significant question guides the reader to understand that chemical products could be monitored for quality and precision at any point of time during the reaction process.

While the answer to the less-significant question may be interesting, it is not needed to understand the process of chemical reaction the author is explaining. |

assessment of students, their interactions with the text, and the tasks you are requiring of them—in this case a deep analysis of the selected text—can make the text less difficult for them.

You may find the tool in figure 3.1 helpful for planning and organizing potential text-dependent questions for a close reading lesson. Organizing questions by type may help you access questions based on students' areas of need more quickly during a lesson.

Type of Question	Text-Dependent Question	Purpose of Question
General Understanding		
Key Details		
Text Structure		
Author's Purpose		
Inferences		
Intertextual Connections		
Vocabulary		

Figure 3.1: Text-dependent question planning chart.

Visit **go.SolutionTree.com/literacy** for a free reproducible version of this figure.

Decision 4: Plan Your Implementation for the Close Reading

Before sharing the text with your students, it's important to plan your implementation and management of the lesson. To do so, there are several questions you must consider.

Who Is Doing the Reading?

Since students in grades K–2 are not yet fluent readers, teachers in these grades will need to read the selected text and invite them to closely think along with you. When presenting the close reading to students in grades 3–12, you may decide that students will do the initial reading independently. Subsequent readings can either be done independently, by table partners, by you, or by some combination of these. If, as you observe annotations and listen in on partner talk, you notice there's a lack of understanding occurring because students aren't reading fluently or their inability to pronounce topical language is interfering with their analyzing of the passage, you will want to take a turn reading the text. Remember, you are just doing the reading and allowing the students to do the analysis.

Does Any Front-Loading Need to Occur?

Very little front-loading of information should occur during a close reading because we often underestimate a reader's base of knowledge and also his or her ability to apply reading skills that help him or her independently unlock the text's meaning. We want to allow students to have opportunities to do the analysis. However, this doesn't mean that we will leave our students to struggle with a text. You may determine that a text does not include the context needed to allow students to define a certain word, and you may need to define it up front. This is your decision, and it is based on an understanding of your students and the text. If you aren't totally sure, you may want to invite the first reading to give students a chance to define the word or grasp a concept, and then provide the information if it is still needed. Only define a word or add unknown information as a scaffold if there is not sufficient context to allow students to glean the meaning.

You might also decide that your students don't have enough background knowledge to allow them to do a deep analysis of the text. Again you might ask an initial question to assess general understanding, and if you determine that students are not able to understand because of limited background knowledge, you might briefly share the context before continuing. This is a delicate balance because you do not want to share so much information that you do the analysis for your students. You want to give students the opportunity to struggle a bit so that they will have the opportunity to use all their skills and the strategies they have been taught to understand the text while also building their stamina.

Rather than front-loading information unnecessarily, as you'll see in the examples we provide throughout this text, teachers backfill the information through the questions they ask, the opportunities they provide for partner collaboration, and the subsequent instruction they provide.

How Many Times Should You Plan to Revisit the Text?

The number of times you revisit the text depends on the areas of complexity you have identified. The areas of difficulty you note and the corollary questions you plan will determine the number of times the class will need to reread the complex text. You will probably first ask a question that causes students to glean a general understanding of the text. Then perhaps you'll ask one question for each area of complexity. Your questions should push students to look at a specific part of the text. Remember that each time students return to the text, they do not need to reread the entire work. By returning to only a small portion, multiple rereads can be accomplished during one lesson. Again, each reread should focus on an area you initially identified as being one of complexity.

When planning your close reading, be sure that you have determined how many times the text will be read and who will do the reading. This, of course, may change once you begin, but it initially provides you an organizational security.

How Should the Text Be Chunked or Numbered?

Identifying the text chunks supports your question asking as well as the students' responses because everyone knows exactly where to look. It allows teachers and students to quickly identify specific sections or lines in the text when the teacher or students refer to them. Be sure to make the decision about the chunking and numbering of the text before starting the first reading. As you ask students to reread, you may only want them to return to a paragraph to look at a particular phrase or to look at specific lines in a specific paragraph to identify a particular structure the author used. You want students to have numbered the passage so that they can easily refer to a segment from which they have gained information or need clarity.

What Annotations Should Students Use?

Before you begin the process of asking students to closely read texts, you will want to have identified a common class set of annotation marks. Annotations are very useful in slowing down the reader and inviting notation of one's thinking while reading. They help readers to focus on the information the text is sharing. Mortimer Adler and Charles Van Doren (1972) suggest that some common annotation marks include circling key words, highlighting confusing words, underlining major points, recording questions and perhaps answers in the margins, numbering a series of information on the page being read or on other related pages, or drawing vertical lines to enclose statements that are too large to underline or highlight. You may wish to add annotations as needed. You may also want to create a chart that shows these annotations or others that you and your colleagues agree to use. Figure 3.2 shows an example of an annotation chart that is appropriate for use with students in the primary grades, and figure 3.3 shows an example of an annotation chart for the upper grades. Notice how these annotations become more extensive and sophisticated in the upper grades.

Figure 3.2: Primary grades annotation chart.

Annotate--"talk" to the text
→ (don't forget your margin notes)

- number your paragraphs or chunks of text
- underline major points
- box confusing words
- circle key words/phrases
- "?" questions
- "!" surprises
- connect information
- [ ] author's claim

Figure 3.3: Upper grades annotation chart.

During the close reading, you may want to ask students to use only one annotation to address a particular question, for example, underlining the argument the author is making, highlighting the cause of the problem, or circling language that is confusing.

While annotations help readers to slow down while reading and to make notations of their thinking, your directions when teaching the annotations should be to encourage students to concentrate more on the information being shared than on their use of annotations. While reading informational or literary texts, students should mark or annotate directly on the text. If they are reading a section of their textbook, you may want to have them write on a plastic sheet that can be reused.

Students need to be taught how to annotate a text through modeling. This can occur easily as you think aloud about a text and annotate the important points. It's important to encourage consistency so that students will begin to use annotations automatically as they read across the disciplines. We have found that if students number the paragraphs, they have an easier time referencing the text as they discuss their thinking with a partner or call into question a confusing area. Figure 3.4 (page 66) shows an annotated text from a fourth grader to whom a teacher has just introduced annotation. His teacher suggested students underline major ideas and also write their questions in the margin to improve their comprehension.

The teacher used a chart similar to the one in figure 3.2 that did not contain too many annotations, but she also included an arrow, like the one in figure 3.3, to remind the students to specifically focus on one area of annotation. Each time she introduced a new area for focus, she moved the arrow to emphasize the new focus area.

Ricky

Bud, Not Buddy - - - Chapter 1

1

??

Why
would
someone
get
paddled?
hit?

HERE WE GO AGAIN. We were all standing in line waiting for breakfast when one of the caseworkers came in and tap-tap-tapped down the line. Uh-oh, this meant <u>bad news</u>, either <u>they'd found a foster home for somebody or somebody was about to get paddled.</u> All the kids watched the woman as she moved along the line, her high-heeled shoes sounding like little fire- crackers going off on the wooden floor.

Shoot! She stopped at me and said, "Are you Buddy Caldwell?"

I said, "It's Bud, not Buddy, ma'am." — **? Why is this the title of book?**

She put her hand on my shoulder and took me out of line. Then she pulled Jerry, one of the littler boys, over. "Aren't you Jerry Clark?" He nodded.

2

"Boys, good news! Now that the school year has ended, you both have been <u>accepted in new temporary- care homes starting this afternoon!</u>"

Jerry asked the same thing I was thinking. "Together?"

She said, "Why, no. Jerry, you'll be in a family with three little girls ..."

Jerry looked like he'd just found out they were going to dip him in a pot of boiling milk.

3

". .. and Bud ..." She looked at some papers she was holding. "Oh, yes, the Amoses, you'll be with Mr. and Mrs. Amos and <u>their son, who's twelve years old, that makes him just two years older than you, doesn't it, Bud?</u>"

??
Is this
Bud's
new
family?

"Yes, ma'am."

She said, "I'm sure you'll both be very happy." **want to be**

Me and Jerry looked at each other.

They aren't
happy. Do they
want to be
together?

4

The woman said, "Now, now, boys, no need to <u>look so glum.</u> I know you don't understand what it means, but there's a depression going on all over this country. People can't find jobs and these are very, very difficult times for everybody. We've been lucky enough to find two wonderful families who've opened their doors for you. I think it's best that we show our new foster families that we're very ..."

??
What's
that
mean?
Sad, I
think.

Figure 3.4: Fourth-grade annotation sample.
Source: Adapted from Curtis, 1999, pp. 1–2.

In contrast, Estrella, a seventh-grade student who had been closely reading and annotating for two years, annotated figure 3.5 (page 68). She was very experienced with the process. When asked how text annotation helped her, she said, "It really helps me when I am reading a text that I don't understand real well. I'm glad we can annotate when we need to because sometimes I don't need to do it as much." When asked what makes the difference, she said, "If it's hard for me, I like to annotate because it helps me to really focus." As with any other skill, once you are confident that students know how and why to annotate, they should be allowed to use it as they feel it is needed. However, if you observe that students are not comprehending and not annotating, you may need to encourage them to annotate. You may wish to review the annotation symbols, or you may need to reteach and model annotation to a small group of students.

What Types of Student Talk Should Occur During the Close Reading?

To answer this question, you'll need to think about how much time you have for the analysis of the selected text. Then you can decide what configuration to use for student conversations about the text. Configurations may include partner talk, table talk, and whole-class talk. In addition to determining the group configurations for the collaborative talk, you'll need to decide how many times collaboration will occur. When making this decision, remember that collaborative talk is a very important part of close reading because it is during this time that students share and expand their understanding of the text, and it allows you to assess how well your students are analyzing and comprehending the material.

What Types of Differentiation Will Occur Throughout the Close Reading?

To begin, you might plan table or partner groups that contain both fluent and developing English learners (ELs) so that language support is available to them. Heterogeneously group students so that everyone has opportunities to grow from rich text analysis and collaborative conversations. As you circulate among students, you may also offer additional prompts or ask additional scaffolded questions to promote understanding for a student who is struggling. And on the conclusion of the close reading, you can provide differentiated scaffolding for individuals who need additional instruction to ensure their understanding of the text.

What Resources Are Necessary?

If students are reading a subsection of their textbooks, decide in advance if you will need plastic covers or sticky notes for annotations. If you are using colored pens or markers, have them readily available. If the text is being shown on a document camera or whiteboard, ensure it is set up ahead of time. You do not want to delay or interfere with the close reading due to a technical problem.

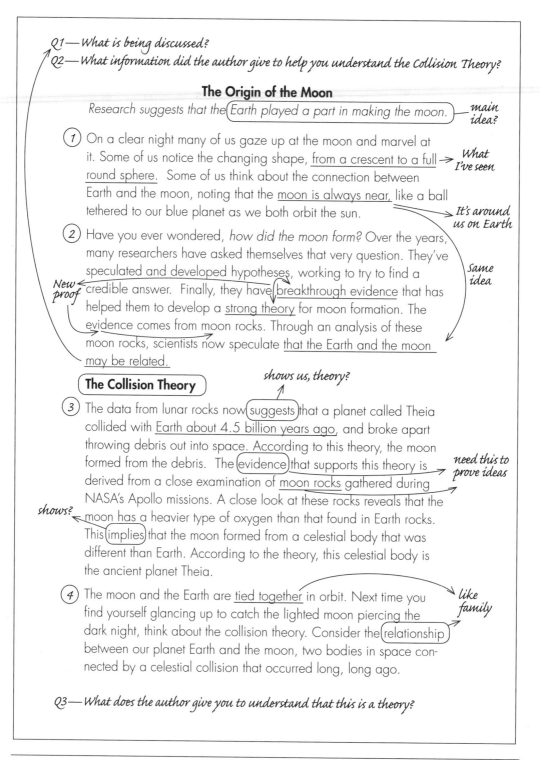

Figure 3.5: Seventh-grade annotation sample.

When Will You Model the Close Reading Process?

Before engaging students in a close reading, model for them the behaviors such as rereading, annotating, and partner collaboration that are associated with close reading and also explain the positive effects that close reading has on comprehension. Explain that being a great reader will improve their ability to get into college or to get a good job. This mindfulness is empowering to students. Once they understand both the purpose and practice of close reading, you can invite them to practice close reading whenever it meshes with your lesson purpose.

Do Students Like Close Reading?

Close reading is a skill that all students should know how to use to support their comprehension. We asked students in grades 4–12 how they felt about the process of close reading. The following is what a few said.

- Alan, grade 4: "It takes more time but it helps me know more about what we're reading."

- Inez, grade 6: "I gotta really take my time. Annotating helps me take more time."

- Ruthie, grade 9: "The readings are usually too long. That's what I don't like. What I do like is that close reading helps me understand the text more. The annotations and rereading help me figure out the meaning. You have to read slow and carefully."

- David, grade 11: "I don't like how long it takes and how much effort I have to put into it. But, I do like that it's a challenge and when I'm done and I figure out the meaning of the reading, I'm proud of myself. I feel like I accomplished something."

It's interesting that the insights of these students regarding close reading summarizes well Brummett's (2010) idea that close reading is a "mindful, disciplined reading of an object [text] with a view to deeper understanding of its meanings" (p. 9) that we believe should be a process taught to all students to support their abilities to deeply analyze texts.

Should You Abandon a Complex Text?

The text-dependent questions the teacher asks during close reading, the rereadings with annotations that a reader completes, and the conversations that occur among classmates should provide the scaffolds that most readers need to master a text or section of text chosen to help achieve the lesson purpose. Therefore, the answer to this question is a simple one: No. Rather than abandon a complex text that presents a challenge for students, teachers should draw from strategies previously taught during guided reading to scaffold instruction of complex texts. During a close reading, many students may instinctually apply strategies they have been taught during guided reading instruction. For example, prior to beginning the initial complex text reading, students may preview the text and look at bold words, subtitles, pictures, and graphs to get a sense of what to anticipate; they might think about what they already know about the topic; they may set a purpose for reading, and while reading they may stop to reread if they find that they are unable to understand. You should not explicitly direct students to engage in these practices *before* beginning a close reading. However, these are strategies that readers often use, so they may occur automatically.

During a close reading, it would absolutely help if students used these strategies, but not at the teacher's prodding. The goal of close reading is that all readers become metacognitively aware of their own reading so that they can automatically apply needed strategies as a way to support their comprehension. If during a close reading with elementary-aged students, you notice they are not engaged and are not applying these strategies, you can revisit the strategies during guided reading instruction. With upper-grades students, who are not involved in guided reading instruction, you can introduce or encourage the use of a particular reading strategy when meeting with a small group that has shown a need for contingent scaffolding. Teaching these strategies should not be a dimension of introducing the initial close reading. However, you may have to reintroduce them for students who still struggle following close reading. These skills, which you share as differentiated scaffolds, may be ones that help them master the complexity of the text.

Conclusion

You must make each of these decisions with your attention focused on your students. You will need to initially consider students' cognitive capabilities and experiences as you identify the areas of text complexity, craft questions, and identify your management plan. During the lesson, you will assess their developing understandings as they respond to the text-dependent questions you ask, annotate their texts, and engage in collaborative conversations. From the initial planning until the conclusion of the close reading lesson, you will be involved in a cycle of continuous assessment that will support the decisions you make about selecting the text, developing the text-dependent questions you'll ask, the progress each student will make toward deep understanding, the extension tasks that will provide students opportunities to share and expand their knowledge, and the small-group contingencies you'll need to design for students striving toward text comprehension.

Your assessment helps identify the students who have a deep understanding of the text and those who need differentiated scaffolds. This information will help you craft extension tasks, which some students can begin immediately while others meet with you for a bit more instruction before they participate in the extension tasks. Close reading success is dependent on close and continuous assessment of both your students and your instruction. In the next chapter, we'll examine specifics of how you can conduct formative assessments throughout a close reading lesson.

4

Assessing During Close Reading

Teachers who are focused on their students develop a good idea of their students' range of existing literacy skills and disciplinary knowledge strengths and needs. They notice the learning that is occurring for their students, and they act on these observations. It is this knowledge that provides the basis for instructional planning. These teachers first identify the instructional purpose, then they plan instruction intended to support students accomplishing that purpose, and then during instruction they continually collect evidence that helps them identify the students who understand well enough to accomplish the lesson purpose as well as those who do not. They gain these insights by watching students as they participate in class discussions, share their written and oral work, self-initiate study of topics that interest them, and select texts for independent reading. They continually assess, and the inferences they make based on the data they collect inform their next instructional steps. This continuous assessment is often referred to as *formative assessment*, which is assessment *for* learning and occurs throughout the teaching and learning experience. It is unlike *summative assessment*, which is assessment *of* learning and occurs after the teaching and learning have concluded. It follows that formative assessments are most helpful when applied during a close reading, as teachers are able to gauge student learning in real time and make adjustments throughout the lesson to best ensure student understanding and success.

Because students perform differently in different subjects and even when they are studying diverse topics within a subject, continuous observation and assessment of student performance should occur throughout the day in all middle and high school disciplines and elementary classrooms in order to gain an accurate snapshot of each student's strengths and needs. To understand the reality of this differentiated performance, think about how well you might perform reading a text written on a challenging topic you are unfamiliar with, such as complex analysis, quantum mechanics, minimalism, or endogenic and exogenic powers. Your initial performance would depend on your background knowledge of the topic, your understanding of the discipline-related language, your motivation, and your reading skills. Without background knowledge of the topic or language, you may struggle. But with a teacher who anticipates your performance, plans accordingly, and follows the Common Core State Standards guidelines that "instruction should be differentiated," and teachers should "discern when particular children or activities warrant more or less attention," you would most likely be motivated and supported to succeed with any of these foreign topics (NGA & CCSSO, 2010, p. 15). Further addressing the power of paying close attention to students in order to make the next decisions about instruction, educational literacy researcher Marie Clay (2005) notes:

> From the recommended procedures a teacher selects those that she requires for a particular child with a particular problem at a particular moment in time. There are no set teaching sequences: there is no prescription to learn this before that. A highly appropriate recommendation for one child could be an unnecessary one for another child. (p. 2)

This quote captures what differentiated scaffolds should look like when teachers assess continually and formatively. Throughout close reading instruction, the teacher must continually assess learner performance (via responses to questions, contributions to conversations, and annotations) in order to offer instructional scaffolds that enable the learner to succeed. During these scaffolds, teachers will continue to assess students' understanding as they work more closely with the text.

Scaffolds Support Assessment During Close Reading

As we've noted, background knowledge plays a significant role in comprehension. But this doesn't mean students can't learn from a text on a topic about which they have limited knowledge and language. In fact, this is exactly what is being referred to as a complex text—the type of text that requires a close reading involves many returns for rereading. Each return should cause the reader to focus on a specific aspect of the text, with the goal being to expand knowledge and continually deepen comprehension. An expert teacher assesses student understanding, identifying the content and concepts students need to return to, and supports the unraveling of the information contained in the text until a reader learns how to do so independently. To view a video of how a sixth-grade science teacher assesses as her students engage in a close reading, visit http://www.learner.org/courses/readwrite/video-detail/fostering-close-reading.html. Notice how, based on her assessments, which she notes on the note-taking form for whole-group close reading (figure 4.1), she is quickly able to offer a needed scaffold that keeps the entire class engaged in a deepening analysis of the text they are reading about rocks. This video of a sixth-grade class engaging in close reading is one of many videos offered in the series *Reading & Writing in the Disciplines*, which can be accessed on the Annenberg Learner website at www.learner.org.

Continuous Assessment Enables Good Teaching and Learning

Throughout a close reading, as teachers observe students, view their annotations, and listen to their collaborations with peers, they are able to assess how well students have comprehended the layered meanings of the text. Using note-taking charts like the one in figure 4.1 supports the documentation of these on-the-spot assessments. Teachers can

Record student names or initials as well as notes and comments regarding their performance during the close reading. This information will help identify total numbers of students who need instructional scaffolding.

	Meaning (Main ideas, key details)	Structure (Organization, visual supports and layout, relationships, vocabulary)	Language (Style and tone, use, purpose, theme, point of view)	Knowledge Demands (Background knowledge)
First Reading Notes and Comments				
Second Reading Notes and Comments				
Third Reading Notes and Comments				
Fourth Reading Notes and Comments				
	Total:	Total:	Total:	Total:

Figure 4.1: Note-taking form for whole-group close reading.

Visit **go.SolutionTree.com/literacy** for a free reproducible version of this figure.

use such a chart to note areas in which specific students struggle, creating a record of students' needs and progress.

Compiling this information during the close reading provides a quick overview regarding students' understanding of the text's meaning, the structures the author uses to convey meaning, the style and use of language, and the cultural and topical foundations of the text. Students whose names or initials appear on this chart are those who need contingent scaffolds to support their understanding of the text. (Teachers may choose to record names or initials, depending on which method is faster and clearer for them.)

Those not listed on the chart have understood the text and are ready for extension tasks that provide them opportunities to apply and extend what they have learned. These insights provide teachers the information they need to ask a next question or offer a prompt that scaffolds learning by drawing students' attention to a particular segment or text feature. Teachers also use information they are gaining to identify which students may need additional small-group differentiated scaffolds once the whole-class close reading concludes. This information can be recorded on a chart similar to the one shown in figure 4.2. These very focused scaffolds support students' close analysis of a targeted text.

Meaning	Structure	Language	Knowledge Demands
Students: Instruction:	Students: Instruction:	Students: Instruction:	Students: Instruction:

Figure 4.2: Note-taking form for next steps for small-group close reading.
Visit **go.SolutionTree.com/literacy** for a free reproducible version of this figure.

The following section provides an example of how one teacher assesses during close reading and differentiates and provides scaffolding based on her assessment data. Notice how she uses the note-taking forms we've shared (figures 4.1 and 4.2) to assess students while listening to their responses to text-dependent questions and peer conversations and observing their annotations. Visit **go.SolutionTree.com/literacy** to access an appendix with additional examples of other grade levels and disciplines.

Grade 8 Social Studies Example

In this example, we observe Karen Shamir, who is planning a close reading of the complex text *Transcript of President Andrew Jackson's Message to Congress 'On Indian Removal' (1830)* (Our Documents, n.d.). The social studies class is studying Native American removal. Her lesson purpose is to have students determine whether the actions of President Jackson were supportive of American Indians and whether the westward expansion was justified.

Notice in table 4.1 that she designs many questions to support students' analysis of what the text says, how it works, and what it means. She designs multiple questions to use as scaffolds to support her students' deep analysis of the text. Since she can't totally

Table 4.1: Ms. Shamir's Text-Dependent Question Examples

Type of Question	Text-Dependent Question	Purpose of Question
General Understanding	What is President Jackson's message about?	To focus readers on the general idea that Jackson was justifying Native American removal to Congress
Key Details	How did Jackson explain the "pecuniary advantages" of his removal plan?	To guide students toward an understanding of Jackson's point of view or opinion
Text Structure	How does Jackson use questions and answers (his own answers) to make his points?	To focus students on the use of questions and answers, as a text structure rooted in persuasion, to sway opinion
Author's Purpose	Why is Jackson writing to Congress?	To make students aware of the persuasive nature of the message
Inferences	Jackson starts out saying he is announcing to Congress that he has a "benevolent policy." Do all parts of his speech indicate that his policy is benevolent? Explain your thinking.	To guide students toward an understanding of the one-sidedness (single perspective) of the text by having them notice sentences such as, "What good man would prefer a country covered with forests and ranged by a few thousand savages to our extensive Republic, studded with cities, towns, and prosperous farms embellished with all the improvements which art can devise or industry execute, occupied by more than 12,000,000 happy people, and filled with all the blessings of liberty, civilization and religion?"; students may identify that Jackson was calling the Native Americans savages, while simultaneously saying that removal was benevolent
Intertextual Connections	Recall the letter by John Ross, principal chief of the Cherokee Nation from 1828–1866, we read two days ago (Cherokee Nation, n.d.). Does the letter convey the same or different ideas than Jackson's message? Explain your thinking.	To move students toward an understanding of the rhetorical nature of Jackson's message—his speech contradicts the sentiments and experiences of Chief John Ross (students should note lines from Ross' letter such as, "We are overwhelmed! Our hearts are sickened, our utterance is paralized, when we reflect on the condition in which we are placed, by the audacious practices of unprincipled men, who have managed their stratagems with so much dexterity as to impose on the Government of the United States, in the face of our earnest, solemn, and reiterated protestations" [Cherokee Nation, n.d.])

predict their initial success, this preparation helps her to be ready for whatever she assesses as she watches and listens to her students. She realizes that she may not need to ask every question but has them just in case.

Even with all of this preparation and scaffolding, Ms. Shamir knows there might be a small group of students who will not deeply comprehend this complex text. Once she assesses why they were not able to deeply analyze the text, she will determine the next steps or instructional contingencies to support these students. At the conclusion of the close reading, she will also decide the next steps for the larger group of students who mastered this text. She often invites students to identify how they would like to extend the knowledge they learned, or if there is a specific sequence of learning that needs to occur on the topic, she plans an extension lesson. For this lesson, she decides that she would like to have the students write an argumentative essay identifying whether they believe President Jackson's actions favored Native Americans and therefore justified westward expansion. Like Ms. Shamir did, at the conclusion of a close reading, teachers must decide the next instructional steps for both the larger group and for any smaller groups. These decisions are based on data gathered throughout the close reading.

For the first close reading, students address the general understanding question, What is President Jackson's message about? Following this reading, Ms. Shamir listens to partner talk and uses her note-taking chart (figure 4.3) to document the needs of students who seem unsure or confused in the areas of meaning, structure, language, and knowledge demands. Notice that she assesses and notes student data as they read and collaborate. The data she records identify the areas where specific students need scaffolds to support their understanding. She also notes which students need contingency scaffolds in these same areas. These students are the ones she will meet with in a small-group configuration if they are not able to unlock understandings through a series of text-dependent questions and partner talk.

The second close reading involves students addressing the key detail question, How did Jackson explain the "pecuniary advantages" of his removal plan? Again, after this close reading, Ms. Shamir listens as students discuss the question. She notes those students who struggle with concepts by again recording it on her chart (figure 4.3). Language is a significant issue for some students.

Following this, Ms. Shamir strategically focuses students on the author's purpose—an area she deems necessary for understanding Jackson's subtle yet purposeful intent when writing the document. She asks, "Why is Jackson writing to Congress?" Ms. Shamir hopes that an understanding of Jackson's purpose might reveal more about the ironic use of terms like *benevolent*. After reading, students discuss the question—some noting that President Jackson had a reason. As Johnny explains, "He wanted the Native Americans gone." A few students are still confused by the text's language as indicated by their responses during the discussion. For example, when asked to answer the question, Why is Jackson writing to Congress?, one student stated that "He wanted to help the Native Americans stay where they were." Ms. Shamir notes the students having difficulty on her chart.

Text: _Transcript of Pres. Andrew Jackson's message to Congress_ Literary __ Informational _x_

Lexile: _1050_   Grade: _8_   Date: _Feb. 17_

Whole-Group Close Reading

Record student names or initials as well as notes and comments, and calculate total numbers of students needing scaffolding.

	Meaning (Main ideas, key details)	**Structure** (Organization, visual supports and layout, relationships, vocabulary)	**Language** (Style and tone, use, purpose, theme, point of view)	**Knowledge Demands** (Topical, cultural)
First Reading Notes and Comments	R.G., M.C., C.R. Annotations: What does that mean?		L.W., R.G., D.G., M.C., B.R., A.G., C.P.	
Second Reading Notes and Comments	M.C., C.R.	R.M., S.T.	L.W., R.G., M.C., B.R., A.G., C.P. Annotations: Question marks next to words	L.W., R.G., A.G.
Third Reading Notes and Comments	C.R. said, "I still don't get what he's saying."		L.W., R.G., B.R., C.P., Conversation: Students don't know the term _benevolent_	
Fourth Reading Notes and Comments			L.W., R.G., B.R., C.P.	
	Total: 0	Total: 0	Total: 4	Total: 0

Figure 4.3: Ms. Shamir's assessment of students during close reading.   CONTINUED →

Next Steps for Small-Group Close Reading

Meaning	Structure	Language	Knowledge Demands
Students:	Students:	Students: L.W., R.G., B.R., C.P.	Students:
Instruction:	Instruction:	Instruction: *Focus on the words* policy *and* provision. *Model how to determine if these words are viewed positively or negatively.* *Think aloud to show how to use metacognition; use the language of close reading—close thinking, decipher—when talking about the text.*	Instruction:

The fourth reading is intended to guide students toward inferring in preparation for their argument paper. Again, Ms. Shamir hopes that this lens will unlock language meaning as well. Ms. Shamir asks, "Jackson starts out saying he is announcing to Congress that he has a 'benevolent policy.' Do all parts of his speech indicate that his policy is benevolent? Explain your thinking." While many students seem to be able to dig deeply into this text, especially with the support of partner talk, language is still confusing for a few of them. For these students, contingency instruction is the next step. Let's take a closer look at Ms. Shamir's data.

Students R.G., M.C., and C.R., who were struggling with the meaning after the first reading, understand with additional readings and collaboration. Similarly, students R.M., S.T., L.W., R.G., and A.G. were all striving to understand more about the text structure and knowledge demands. However, by the final reading, Ms. Shamir has assessed that those five students did not need additional instruction. Through the question scaffolds she asks and student collaboration, students built the knowledge they needed to understand the content and the structure.

Look closely at the students listed in the Language column. After the initial reading, Ms. Shamir notes that these seven students expressed some confusion with the language either in their annotations or conversations. After the second reading, the number decreases to six. (D.G. is off the list! Ms. Shamir assesses that through peer conversation he understands the words that initially confused him.) After the third reading, students revisit the text, and four students remain on the list. Despite scaffolds of additional text-dependent questions and collaborative conversations, these four students still lack a deep understanding of the text because of their insufficient language knowledge.

Ms. Shamir uses this assessment information to conclude that these students need additional instructional contingencies to support their reading of the text. She also concludes that the majority of students can work on a related but independent task while she works with this smaller group.

Next Steps for the Whole Class

After this close reading, Ms. Shamir asks the larger group that had successfully analyzed the text to use Jackson's statement and other previously read documents to argue in support *of* or *against* westward expansion. For this project, students complete a *Foldable*™ (student-created graphic organizers in which they fold a piece of paper into sections) that documents evidence that supports westward expansion and evidence that opposes westward expansion. After they organize their pros and cons, students utilize a protocol for writing an argument in which they develop a claim, provide text-based evidence from multiple sources that supports the claim, note counterclaims, and restate their claim. Figure 4.4 illustrates the protocol and the sentence frames that Ms. Shamir provided to her students to support their argumentative writing project. While the majority of the students work on this extension task, Ms. Shamir meets with struggling students to offer more guided support.

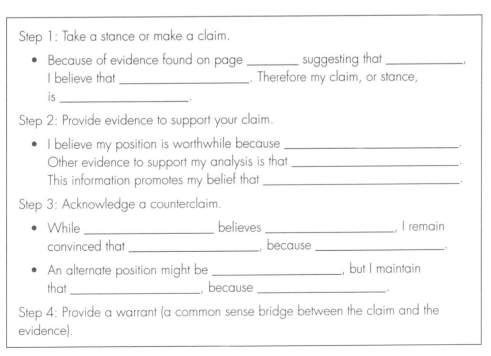

Step 1: Take a stance or make a claim.

- Because of evidence found on page _____ suggesting that _____,
  I believe that _____. Therefore my claim, or stance,
  is _____.

Step 2: Provide evidence to support your claim.

- I believe my position is worthwhile because _____.
  Other evidence to support my analysis is that _____.
  This information promotes my belief that _____.

Step 3: Acknowledge a counterclaim.

- While _____ believes _____, I remain
  convinced that _____, because _____.

- An alternate position might be _____, but I maintain
  that _____, because _____.

Step 4: Provide a warrant (a common sense bridge between the claim and the evidence).

Figure 4.4: Step-by-step sentence frames for argumentative writing.

CONTINUED →

- I believe _____ (claim), because _____
  (evidence) and _____ (common sense warrant).

- Based on my observation that _____ (evidence) and the facts
  that suggest _____ (evidence), I believe _____
  (claim). Furthermore, _____ (common sense warrant) suggests
  that _____ (claim).

- However, _____ (counterclaim), but the facts—namely, _____
  (evidence)—support my original stance that _____ (claim).

Step 5: Summarize your claim.

- To conclude, I maintain that _____. This is a reasonable
  stance because evidence that _____ and _____
  overwhelmingly support the conclusion that _____.

Source: Moss, Lapp, Grant, & Johnson, 2015, p. 153.

Differentiated Scaffolds for a Small Group

Ms. Shamir provides some additional contingencies for the smaller group of students that are designed to address the issues causing the students not to deeply comprehend the language demands and interfering with their deep analysis. For this particular small group, Ms. Shamir realizes that students struggle with complex language that is so commonly seen in social studies texts. Specifically, she wants them to be able to address CCSS.ELA-LITERACY.RH.6-8.4: "Determine the meaning of words and phrases as they are used in a text, including vocabulary specific to domains related to history/social studies" (NGA & CCSSO, 2010). This standard is similar to ones appearing in many state standards that call for students to understand a wide array of language.

Ms. Shamir meets with four students (L.W., R.G., B.R., and C.P.), saying: "Let's go back to this same text to closely read it one more time. This time I want you to notice where Jackson is using social studies words, like *policy* and *provision*. Let's also try to notice how he is describing these social studies words. Notice if he's talking about them in a positive or negative way. For example, in the first sentence Jackson says, 'It gives me pleasure to announce to Congress that the benevolent policy of the Government, steadily pursued for nearly thirty years, in relation to the removal of the Indians beyond the white settlements is approaching to a happy consummation.'

"There are lots of challenging vocabulary words in this sentence. When I read this, I notice *policy* and *Government*. Then I notice that Jackson says 'it gives [him] great pleasure,' and I think to myself, Jackson is happy about this policy and somehow it connects to the US government. I'm not sure what *benevolent* means, but I'm not going to let that stop me from reading. I can still get a sense of what this is about. I can tell that this is about moving the Native Americans from their lands because Jackson mentioned Indian removal, which we have talked about in class. So, you can see that by closely thinking about this sentence, I could figure out, or decipher, the meaning of the sentence by especially paying attention to my social studies words and the descriptive words that surround them. Now it's your turn. Read the next two paragraphs, and annotate the social studies words along with words that help you determine the tone or feelings around these social studies terms. Then we will do some partner talk to discuss our ideas."

Notice that Ms. Shamir decides to stick with the same text because she assessed that this smaller group could master the information through engaging with her in a small-group close reading where her questions further focus them on disciplinary terms that are at the heart of the text meaning. She wants them to get the gist, tone, and connections to history so they can compare Jackson's ideas to other contrary depictions of Native American removal—depictions that discuss the tragedies experienced by the Native Americans as a result of Jackson's policy. With this manner of instruction, Ms. Shamir feels that students will be able to see that Jackson is expressing his opinion in a rhetorical fashion common in such speeches.

She also could have decided to use a less complex partner text with this group to develop vocabulary first, and then progress to the main text. It's important in your preplanning to identify potential paired texts in case your students need additional contingencies. Ms. Shamir selects the book *Westward Expansion and Migration, Grades 6–12* (Barden & Backus, 2011) for this purpose. Her ultimate goal is to ensure that all her students succeeded in reading the complex text, even if she needs to revisit it with them or take the interim step of sharing a less complex text first.

In this case, Ms. Shamir decides to stick with the original complex text and have her small group reread with a focus on topical vocabulary—social studies words—and on the describing words and phrases that indicate tone and feeling. Based on these data, Ms. Shamir crafts her plan to support these students by modeling her own expert thinking using the think-aloud strategy and by strategically focusing on determining the meanings or general sense of unknown words. Ms. Shamir makes thinking aloud a habit in her class. She believes it's the most effective way to show students how she, as the teacher expert, negotiates challenging text to derive meaning. It's important to note that when Ms. Shamir thinks aloud, she makes sure to consider things from the students' perspective. For instance, when Ms. Shamir considers the term *benevolent* during her brief think-aloud, she states that she is not sure about the meaning, but she adds that she will persevere to continue reading in hopes that she could use the context to discover the meaning. In essence, Ms. Shamir is articulating her challenges and her methods for deciphering confusing words, phrases, and parts of the text. She does this in a realistic manner, showcasing struggles and uncertainties while modeling how to overcome them.

Notice, too, that Ms. Shamir chooses to model her thinking in the form of a think-aloud so that students can see what they need to look for. She doesn't do the reading for them, but she makes sure they understand the process and the task. Ultimately, after a think-aloud and additional rereading, coupled with partner talk, Ms. Shamir's group comes to a deeper understanding of Jackson's speech. They can now move to the same argumentative writing task being undertaken by the larger group. At this point, they are ready for it.

Conclusion

Ms. Shamir's exemplar illustrates that the attentive formative assessment teachers conduct by listening in on student talk, observing student work, and evaluating students' answers to questions supplies the data teachers need to identify the next instructional steps for all students—those who accomplished the instructional purpose during the initial close reading and those who need additional contingency scaffolds to support them in accomplishing the lesson purpose. In this classroom, scaffolds in the form of strategically offered text-dependent questions and small-group differentiated instruction provide students with the knowledge they need to move forward in a way that ultimately supports their accomplishment of reading and comprehending the original complex text.

Most teachers are well aware of the wide array of needs in any given classroom. Given the ultimate goal of providing all students with the opportunity to read complex texts, a thoughtful, reflective teacher will use assessment data to make decisions about next steps, and those decisions may vary for different students and groups of students. While collecting this information may seem initially challenging, the benefits are so significant that it is incumbent on all teachers to formatively assess their students and respond by putting scaffolded instruction in place. It will not only be of great benefit to students but will also give teachers a tremendous sense of satisfaction as they see students learning and accomplishing the standards-related lesson purposes.

PART II

INSTRUCTIONAL SCENARIOS

Now that we have explored how to assess which students need initial and contingency scaffolds—and what kinds of scaffolds they need—in the next four chapters we will illustrate how to differentiate scaffolds, with the goal being that all students will acquire the needed language, knowledge, and skills to succeed when closely reading an identified complex text. The primary purpose of these chapters is to share instructional examples featuring differentiated scaffolds designed to support students who do not understand the text during whole-group instruction.

You'll find that some of the scaffolds we discuss appear more than once in the following chapters. For example, you will see the use of questions and think-alouds being used in a variety of examples. This occurs because a teacher can ask different types of questions as scaffolds to support students gaining various types of insights. These questions may pertain, for example, to the language the author is using or the structure of the text being read. This is also true for think-alouds that teachers use to model how to use the context of a few sentences to gain insight about a word the reader doesn't know or how to think about insights drawn from a previously read passage to make sense of a new passage.

The scaffolds shared in these examples can be used with both a whole class and small groups of students. These examples are meant to show how you can employ a sound instructional practice in many situations with a well-focused instructional purpose that is matched to an instructional routine, like thinking aloud or questioning, that offers just the right scaffold to support learning for each student.

You'll see extended examples interspersed throughout the following chapters that illustrate small-group and whole-class instruction occurring at the same time, with one teacher managing it all. We acknowledge that it's tricky to manage both a small group and a whole class simultaneously, but having strong lesson plans that anticipate contingency instruction can be the key.

These differentiated scaffolds are grouped together based on dimensions of text complexity, with each chapter dedicated to a different dimension: what the text says (meaning), how the text works (structure), what the text means (language), and knowledge demands. For each dimension, we illustrate several differentiated-scaffold approaches for students needing additional support.

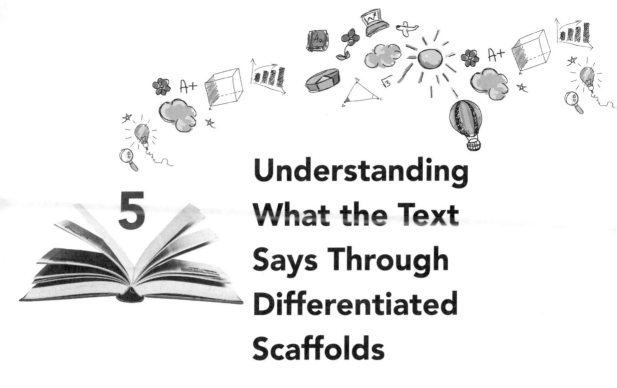

Understanding What the Text Says Through Differentiated Scaffolds

5

Before students can gain a deep understanding of a text's meaning and decide whether or to what degree the information is true, they must have a foundational understanding of the ideas and concepts that are literally stated. They must be able to answer questions such as those Adler and Van Doren (1972) identify: "What is this book about as a whole?" and "What is being said in detail, and how?" (pp. 46–47). Text-based questions teachers and students initially ask during close reading and collaborative conversations throughout the reading help focus students on the basic key ideas and concepts within a text. Questions that focus on the text's language, structure, and meaning stretch the knowledge of the majority of students who, at the conclusion of the close reading, will be ready to use these insights to share and expand their understandings.

Because we know a few students may still need differentiated contingency scaffolds designed to ensure that they will also be successful when closely rereading the text, teachers must decide what scaffolds will help these students gain a basic understanding of the textual information. The contingencies teachers plan should serve as temporary scaffolds to support students in eventually being able to read the initial text and gain an understanding of its meaning. This chapter focuses on the six types of differentiated scaffolds that are designed to enable students to acquire a general understanding of the text and its key details: (1) text-dependent layered questions, (2) graphic organizers, (3) language frames, (4) text chunking, (5) think-alouds, and (6) paired texts. Often explored in a small-group configuration, these scaffolds should push students to revisit the text's meaning as they identify key details and ideas that, when synthesized, provide a general understanding of the text.

Text-Dependent Layered Questions

As noted, effective teachers plan text-dependent questions in advance of a lesson. Through the process of close reading, each subsequent question is intended to move the student deeper than the preceding question. While this is clearly good practice, it is not foolproof. Some teachers find themselves in a quandary when a few students are unable to successfully answer a text-dependent question. This is the point at which *layered* text-dependent questions come into play as an instructional option. Layered text-dependent questions are intended to support students who are unable to answer a particular text-dependent question the teacher has asked. Layered questions focus on the same content that the original text-dependent question addresses, but they scaffold and direct students' attention in a more precise, focused manner. Let's examine layered text-dependent questions in more depth.

Questions for General Understanding

Whether working with the whole class or a smaller group of students, teachers can use focused text-dependent questions to provide a scaffold to information that can support a general understanding of the text. When students have difficulty acquiring a general understanding, they often continue to have difficulties throughout the entire close reading. This happens because they do not have a foundation of information on which to build. Focused questions in a smaller group can help students gain insights on which they can layer deeper understandings. To make this a reality, it is essential that teachers listen to their students' responses and then ask questions that are layered as scaffolded supports on which students can build their understandings. The following questions could be intended for any student; however, the sophistication of the question should increase according to the student's year in school. Questions must also be appropriately challenging for a student's ability level. While the intent of the questions can be similar, cognitive development must be taken into account. If you are teaching primary-grades students, you might begin each question by reminding them to listen as you read and then to use their own words to answer the question. For older students, you will most often ask them to read by themselves and then discuss the answers to questions with partners. These questions help students gain a general understanding of a narrative text.

- **Grade 1:** What is happening in this story?
- **Grade 12:** What are the significant events in this novel?

If students are unable to answer, layered questions would provide the needed scaffolds. Remember each question's complexity should be grade-level appropriate.

For grade 1 students who are unable to answer the general understanding question, the following layered questions provide needed scaffolding.

- What is happening at the beginning of the story?
- What is happening at the end of the story?
- What is this story basically about?

- What does this chunk (*note a section*) mean?

Grade 12 students would be supported by similar layered questions.

- What happened at the beginning to move the story forward?
- What happened at the end to conclude the story?
- What does this section (*note a section*) of the text indicate?
- What problem is (*character name*) encountering? (If students are unable to answer this question, the following four questions would provide layers needed to support answering the initial question. Keep in mind that they might not all need to be asked.)
  a. What is the author telling us about (*character, situation,* or *theme*)?
  b. What is the author telling us about the relationship between (*character*) and (*character*)?
  c. How does (*character*) treat (*character, situation,* or *object*)?
  d. Why is (*character*) angry with (*character, situation,* or *object*)?

Additional layered questions might include the following.

- Which character is this story mostly about?
- Who is the narrator?
- How does the story end?
- Where is the story taking place?

In an informational piece, you might ask questions similar to the following to support readers gaining a general understanding of the information. Again, you should ask layered questions when students are unable to answer the initial question. Listening closely to students' responses helps you in asking just the right question. Even though text-dependent questions can be prepared in advance of the close reading, layered questions should be based on students' responses or anticipated responses.

The following questions support students' understanding of informational text. Note that the specific wording of these questions could be altered to support various grade levels.

- What is the author telling us?
- What subject is being talked about?
- What is the topic being shared?
- What are we learning about this topic?
- What do you already know about this topic?
- What is being described? (If students are unable to answer this question, answering the next two layered questions would provide information for them to use to answer the initial question.)

- ◆ What concerns is the author sharing?
- ◆ When is the topic being presented?
- Where is this event taking place?
- Why does the author repeat the phrase _____?
- Why is the author sharing this information?
- How does the author know this information?

Questions for Key Details

Questions that address key details also help readers identify pieces of information that, when compiled, enable them to better understand the plot, setting, characters, problem, story arc, and solution. Key detail questions about a narrative include the following.

- Who is the main character?
- What are some characteristics of the main character?
- What role does this character play in the story?
- What actions tell you (*name*) is the main character?
- Who are the other characters?
- How do the other characters treat the main character?
- Where does the story take place?
- What is the problem in the story?
- How is the problem solved?

Key detail questions for an informational text can also address the 5Ws (who, what, when, where, and why) and how. Key detail questions for informational texts include the following.

- We just read a section describing (*object*). How many types of (*objects*) exist?
- What are some details about each type of (*object*)?
- What reasons did the author share to make you think that _____?
- What is the author criticizing?
- What concerns does the author have?
- Which (*situations* or *themes*) are similar?
- How are (*situation* or *theme*) and (*situation* or *theme*) different?
- How do the markings of a (*object*) differ from a (*object*)?

These are just a sample of the many questions you can ask to help striving readers retrace key details that will support their gaining a general understanding. Notice how each question is designed to help the reader focus on key pieces of information. General understanding and key detail questions provide the foundation of information that will enable students to eventually comprehend the deep message of the story or text.

The following example illustrates using text-dependent layered questions to support small-group differentiated scaffolding. In Ms. Klinger's second-grade class, students are closely reading "The Boy Who Cried Wolf" (Pinkney, 2000). During the close reading lesson, some of the key detail questions Ms. Klinger asks the students include What is a synonym for sheep in this text? and Where did the boy watch the sheep? Because the majority of the students are able to answer these questions, she continues asking other questions to get at the deeper meaning of the text.

At the end of the close reading lesson, Ms. Klinger is well aware that some students have not grasped the deeper meaning and overall moral of the story and is confident that it is because they are unable to answer some of the key detail questions. Ms. Klinger knows that a brief ten minutes with this group would help them fill in some of the gaps they have about the story. While most of the students research other stories with a similar moral on their tablets, Ms. Klinger calls four students to work with her on the importance of key details and how they can lead to deeper comprehension. She gives her students the analogy of digging a hole, telling them, "Knowing the answers to some key detail questions is like having a bigger, better shovel. It helps you get deeper and discover things you didn't know before. If all you ever use is a small gardening hand shovel, you will only be able to uncover some of the soil. In other words, you will only be able to just scratch the surface."

To fill in some of the gaps the students have, Ms. Klinger revisits some of the initial key detail questions and adds some new ones, including:

- Why did the boy trick the villagers? (He was bored.)
- Why is the setting important in this story? (because the villagers had to come up the mountain, which was a long way)
- What does the author call the boy? (shepherd boy)
- What does the author call the people who live in the village? (villagers)

By asking these key detail questions and giving this small group some more processing time, Ms Klinger helps these students understand the story as a whole.

Graphic Organizers

Graphic organizers, also referred to as *mind maps* and *concept maps*, offer a visual rendition of a topic or concept. They make transparent the multiple dimensions of a challenging concept (Lapp, Wolsey, & Wood, 2015; Lapp, Wolsey, Wood, & Johnson, 2015). Let's consider a few that would work well to support students acquiring a general understanding of the text while identifying key details of a narrative or an informational text.

Graphic Organizer for Informational Texts

Graphic organizers can support students in identifying the main idea and key details that enable them to grasp a general understanding of a text they are reading. While we have seen teachers use main idea and key details graphic organizers with students across all grades when they are reading both narrative and informational texts, we have found them to be especially supportive when reading informational texts. (See figure 5.1, page 90.)

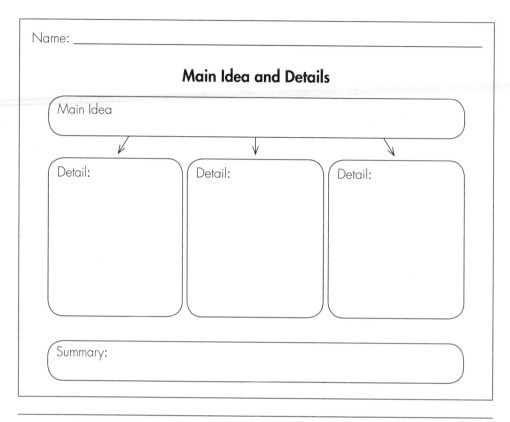

Figure 5.1: Main idea and details graphic organizer.

When working with a smaller group of students to gain a general understanding of the text, begin by inviting the group to first retrace the text so you can identify what students believe might be the main idea. Then model for the students how to search again for pieces of evidence that support their suggestion. Finally, model how to synthesize this information into a summary statement. If the students are unable to do any piece of this independently, model this process for them using a different text, and then have them return to the original text to practice what was modeled.

The following example illustrates using graphic organizers with informational texts to support small-group differentiated scaffolding of the main idea and key details. Jack Coryea and his class of fourth graders are involved in the study of planets. As a close reading, Mr. Coryea invites the students to read *Discovering Mars: The Amazing Story of the Red Planet* by Melvin Berger (1992), a text exemplar in appendix B of the Common Core State Standards (NGA & CCSSO, n.d.b).

After the reading, Mr. Coryea is aware that there are five students who cannot isolate the details in this passage well enough to grasp the vast size of the volcanoes on Mars. He engages the rest of his class in an extension task of investigating other planets to identify if they have volcanoes, when they erupted, if any are currently active, and how they compare in size and number to those on Mars. As this larger group begins this comparative exploration, Mr. Coryea meets with the smaller group and, using this graphic organizer, engages them in the following conversation.

"This is a graphic organizer that I think will help us to untangle the facts in this paragraph. I like to use graphic organizers when I read a text like this that has so much information. The graphic organizer helps me to keep everything straight in my mind. Let's first reread this text to see what big idea the author is talking about," says Mr. Coryea.

Haim (after rereading) adds, "I think it's about how big the volcanoes are on Mars."

"I do too, but there are so many names that I get them mixed up, so I'm not sure," Cindy exclaims.

Marisol says, "Yeah, I think it's about big volcanoes in Mars."

Mr. Coryea questions, "OK, then what should we write on the graphic organizer in the section that says Main Idea?"

Patricia says, "Mars has giant volcanoes. See it says it here (pointing to the second sentence). I saw that before, but then all of the other facts mixed me up."

Darius adds, "OK, let's write 'Mars has giant volcanoes.'"

Mr. Coryea responds, "Terrific, now see if you can go through each sentence and find details to back this up."

After another reread, the students identify the details that support the main idea Patricia suggested. Together they fill them in on the graphic organizer. Then Mr. Coryea asks them to sum up what they have read. Mr. Coryea knows they understand the passage when, after one more reading, Cindy says, "There are giant volcanoes in Mars, and we know how huge they are when their size gets compared to other places like whole states." Darius adds, "It's easy to see with this graphic organizer." These students are now ready to join their peers on the extension task.

Graphic Organizers for Narrative Texts

Graphic organizers for narrative texts can help students to dig deeper into layers of meaning in a text and to engage in analysis that reveals insights of characters' complexity.

Layered-Meaning Graphic Organizer

We especially like layered-meaning graphic organizers, also called *Foldables*, because of their 3-D qualities and also how easy it is for students to create them and then to compile key levels of meaning or detail to arrive at a general understanding of information. To create this Foldable, students cut out rings of construction paper and paste the layers together. We find that when students create Foldables they take greater ownership of the information being noted. Teachers could also use this graphic organizer (see figure 5.2, page 92) when working with students who are reading a narrative that involves uncovering superficial meaning to get to a deeper meaning (story within a story), as in James Thurber's (1942) "The Secret Life of Walter Mitty" or Audrey Niffenegger's (2003) *The Time Traveler's Wife*.

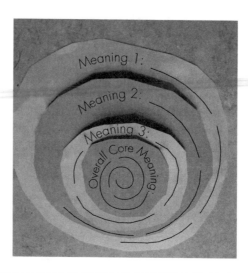

Figure 5.2: Layered-meaning graphic organizer.

The following example illustrates using graphic organizers to support small-group differentiated scaffolding of layers of meaning. In Mr. Cory Greene's eleventh-grade English class, students engage in a close reading of Thurber's (1942) short story "The Secret Life of Walter Mitty." Mr. Greene's purpose for reading this text is to uncover its deepest layers of meaning. His assessment at the conclusion of the final close reading is that most students are able to unravel the story's literal and deeper meaning. They understand that Walter Mitty had five daydreams and know what each entails and means. However, despite Mr. Greene's scaffolds provided through text-dependent questions and whole- and small-group collaborative talk, four students do not understand what the daydreams mean, which suggests they do not comprehend the layers of meaning in this text. Mr. Greene knows that small-group instruction is necessary to provide differentiated scaffolds.

Most students, however, are ready to extend their understanding of the text by examining the character's name, Mitty, and its adjective, *Mittyesque*. The extension activity Mr. Greene presents comes from the students themselves, after one student makes the comment during the lesson, "That's a weird name. I wonder what it means." Mr. Greene is thrilled to hear students taking such an active stance in their learning. He knows this is the perfect time to allow their curiosities to drive the next phase of this lesson. Students use the Internet to learn more about the unique name and apply that knowledge to their understanding of the text—yet another layer of meaning, indeed! As the majority of the class works in pairs to complete this analysis, Mr. Greene turns his attention to the four students who do not understand the multiple layers of meaning. He begins by modeling how he thinks about the first of Mitty's daydreams.

"I know he's flying a navy airplane, but what could that mean on a deeper level? Could a navy pilot be in combat? I wonder if Mitty feels like he is fighting something or someone. Perhaps his wife, who seems to be annoying him. Maybe Mitty is trying to escape and is in conflict with his life."

Mr. Greene fills out the graphic organizer's first layer of onion by writing about the idea of escape and conflict with his own life. "Let's try to do what I just did together as we analyze Mitty's second daydream. First we will talk about what we know about his daydream and then take some of those ideas and see if they are symbols for other things." Students are eager to complete the visual with the layers (meaning), which helps them visualize how each layer builds to a deeper core understanding of versions of Mitty's reality.

As the small group progresses with this process and students have documented the idea that Mitty is trying to escape, James suggests that the story is just about a guy who runs mundane errands with his wife, noting, "He's just like us, a normal guy, but he makes mistakes sometimes." Mr. Greene acknowledges this, and students add it to the graphic organizer. As the story progresses, the reader sees that Mitty has created numerous exciting fantasies for himself. He is a daydreamer who imagines himself in exotic, highly unusual places—a surgical ward, courtrooms, and even in a military dugout. Together, with Mr. Greene guiding, the students investigate each of these fantasies. With more rereading, the four students determine that Walter Mitty, because of his fantasies, has the capacity to enjoy life even when doing common everyday tasks. Deeper analysis of this story reveals a third meaning: Walter Mitty's fantasy world is being defeated by reality. Students consider and identify multiple meanings in the story as they work together to create a layered-meaning graphic organizer for this text. (See figure 5.3.)

Figure 5.3: Layered-meaning graphic organizer example for Walter Mitty.

Character Analysis Graphic Organizer

Analysis of a character leads to a deepening understanding of the story. As the reader comes to understand characters and their relationships to each other, the story layers begin to unfold. The following graphic organizer (figure 5.4, page 94) is one that works well to help readers identify the physical features of a character, the language he or she uses, his or her responses to other characters and situations, and how characters' actions propel the actions of other characters. Readers should provide specific examples from the text and identify the page source. After completing this chart, students should use the collected information to write a description of the character. The identified character features eventually lead the reader to a deepening understanding of not just this character but of his or her relationship to others, and also the story.

Text Title and Author: _____

Character: _____

1. Is the character a protagonist (main character) or antagonist (one who complicates the plot and opposes the protagonist)? _____

2. How do you know? (Share Information from the text.)

3. Use the following table to detail what you've learned about this character.

Physical features	p. _____	p. _____	p. _____
Language What _____ says	p. _____	p. _____	p. _____
Interactions How _____ responds and interacts	p. _____	p. _____	p. _____
Behaviors How_____ acts	p. _____	p. _____	p. _____

4. Because of the actions of _____, my general understanding is that _____ is _____.

Figure 5.4: Graphic organizer for narrative text.
Visit **go.SolutionTree.com/literacy** for a free reproducible version of this figure.

The following example illustrates using graphic organizers to support small-group differentiated scaffolding for character analysis in a narrative text. When third-grade teacher Bonnie Franz chooses a section of the book *Boundless Grace* (Hoffman & Binch, 2000) as a close reading for her students, she knows that some of the ways in which the author develops Grace, the main character, will be tricky for her students. However, Mrs. Franz believes that through a rich discussion with both tablemates and peers in the whole class, students would understand Grace's character traits. As the whole-class close reading is drawing to a close, three students need some differentiated scaffolds to help their meaning making. Before calling these students to her table, Mrs. Franz challenges the rest of the class to use multiple texts to get an even deeper understanding of the character Grace, saying, "You know about Grace from reading this text, *Boundless Grace*, and from reading *Amazing Grace* last week. Make an interactive graphic organizer with your close reading partner to organize your thoughts about some of the similarities and differences you learned about Grace between the two books. Think about how your understanding of Grace deepened with Mary Hoffman's second book."

While the students who comprehend the lesson create their graphic organizer and organize their thoughts across multiple texts, Mrs. Franz quietly taps three students on the shoulder and asks them to come with her so they can more deeply examine Grace's character. She gathers the students discreetly because she does not want to interrupt the others, and she also does not want to call attention to this small group. Mrs. Franz presents the students with a graphic organizer (see figure 5.4), which is copied on large legal-sized paper. Together, students revisit parts of the text and organize their thoughts using the chart as a shared scaffold. Each student has a different colored pencil and fills in parts of the chart as a shared experience. Mrs. Franz gives a copy of selected passages to all three students. Through the following conversation, the students begin to make meaning and understand how Grace develops as a character.

Mrs. Franz says, "Let's look at the illustrations and see what we learn about Grace by her physical features. Pay attention to what you see."

"She likes to talk on the phone; see here on page 18 she is talking on the phone," replies Myra.

Calista asks, "Who is she talking to?"

Mrs. Franz answers, "OK, but look more closely. What clues does the author or illustrator give you to help you understand Grace as a person?"

"Do you mean how she looks in the face?" Manuel further questions.

Mrs. Franz says, "Great detective work. Keep going, Manuel."

Manuel says, "I don't think she looks very happy, even though on the page before she does look happy. Maybe when she is in Africa with that brother and sister, she is happy."

"Oh yes, and when she talks to her ma at home, she is sad," offers Calista.

Myra says, "That makes sense. She is homesick. I can see it in her face, and the author wrote about that right here."

Mrs. Franz is very happy to see how quickly students are understanding the character's development. She is confident that the graphic organizer and small-group scaffolded instruction are allowing the once-struggling students to understand Grace as a character—just as well as the others in the class.

After taking a careful look at the physical characteristics of Grace, Manuel comments that "She looks different in those two pages and also says different things." Mrs. Franz knows that this was a perfect time to direct her students to the second row of the chart to examine Grace's words in these two pages of complex text.

Myra says, "We know she's a happy girl. Here it says she tells bedtime stories . . ."

Manuel says, "Yes, but on this page she talks about feeling like gum, stretched out all thin in a bubble."

Calista responds, "That's gross. She feels like bubble gum."

Mrs. Franz says, "Remember, you already said she was homesick and used the evidence from the illustrations and text to point that out. What do Grace's words tell you about her?"

"Right here after the gum part she says she can't manage two families. She says, 'What if I burst?'" says Myra.

Mrs. Franz says, "Keep going Myra. You're on to something."

Myra adds, "The bursting part reminds me of gum and when you blow a bubble. These two families are so far apart."

Manuel contributes, "One is in Africa and the other is in America, I think."

"Yes, and she says she can't manage them—the two families. It's hard to be a part of both," Myra responds.

Calista says, "Like a bubble you blow with gum. It could pop."

Myra and Manuel both add, "Yes, it could burst."

Calista says, "So is she saying being a part of two families is hard? I think so because Grace says 'there isn't enough of me to go around.'"

Mrs. Franz smiles, and before she can say a word the three students, each with different-colored pencils, are filling in the chart with direct quotes and page numbers to support their meaning making. The chart is being completed quickly, as Mrs. Franz predicted. Figure 5.5 shows students' sample work within the graphic organizer.

Mrs. Franz did not need to do much explicit teaching with this group. She provided the scaffold they needed and asked a few guiding questions to get the students on track. However, she realized that these students needed the visual representation, more time, and the prior knowledge from the whole-class close reading to access the same complex text as the rest of the class. After this interaction Myra, Calista, and Manuel are empowered and confident about this text. Their cognitive lightbulbs have gone on, and closely reading this passage a few additional times with differentiated scaffolds made all the difference in the world.

Text Title and Author: _Boundless Grace by Mary Hoffman_

Character: _Grace_

1. Is the character a protagonist (main character) or antagonist (one who complicates the plot and opposes the protagonist)? _Protagonist_

2. How do you know? (Share Information from the text.)

    The book title includes the character's name, Grace, and Grace is featured on every page. The story is told from Grace's point of view.

3. Use the following table to detail what you've learned about this character.

Physical features	p. 17—Grace is happy when she tells stories to her brother and sister.	p. 18—Grace is homesick when she talks to her ma.	p. Pictures on lots of pages—she is Black and has braids.
Language What _Grace_ says	p. 17—Grace tells bedtime stories. That makes her happy and feel helpful.	p. 18—Grace says "there isn't enough of me to go around"—she is going to burst. she is sad.	p. 18—Grace says "I feel like gum, stretched out all thin in a bubble"—she can't be a part of both families.
Interactions How _Grace_ responds and interacts	pp. 17 & 18—she has lots of different feelings.	p. 5—Grace is worried that her Dad won't love her.	p.
Behaviors How _Grace_ acts	p. 1—Grace misses her Dad.	p. 2—she loves her cat.	p.

4. Because of the actions of _Grace_, my general understanding is that _Grace_ is _the protagonist. she is the main character, and the story is about her wanting to get to be with her dad._

Figure 5.5: Sample graphic organizer for narrative text.

Language Frames

Sentence and paragraph _language frames_ are partially constructed sentences and paragraphs that provide a model of the syntax and vocabulary that allow speakers to share ideas and information in an academic way. Language frames serve as models to get students familiar with how to use academic discourse. Students, especially English learners, often struggle with how to share ideas in an academic way. Sentence or paragraph frames provide a structure to get them started. (See figure 5.6.)

Physical

- From the clues I found on page _____ and page _____ I think _____ looks like _____.

- I agree, and I also found information on page _____ that suggests _____ looks like _____.

Dialogue

- On page _____, _____ says _____. It made me think that _____ because _____.

Responses and Interactions

- _____'s response to _____, which was stated on page _____, gave me the insight that _____.

Actions

- As suggested by the descriptions on page _____ and page _____, the actions of _____ indicate _____.

Conclusion

- Based on these details, I conclude that _____ is _____. My conclusion is most strongly supported by information on page _____ that says that _____.

Figure 5.6: Language frame.

When offering a contingency scaffold to a smaller group of students to help them gain a general understanding of a text, you may want to share the language frames shown in figure 5.6 along with the graphic organizer shown in figure 5.5 to help the students better convey their analysis. These language frames support students discussing the key details they've noted about characters. They also support them using academic language to share their thoughts about an informational text they are reading. You may want to have students first write their thoughts within the context of the language frame. Doing so will develop students' written and oral proficiencies as they identify and share key details about characters in a text they are analyzing. Be sure to remember that language frames are scaffolds that should also be removed once students own the language patterns.

The following example illustrates using language frames to support small-group differentiated scaffolding. Kindergartners in Peggy Aitkens's classroom are learning to use what she calls "school talk," or *academic language*, when they engage in conversations about texts they have closely read. In between each close reading of Nikki Giovanni's (1996) poem "Covers," Miss Aitkens asks her students to talk to their elbow partners about a designated text-dependent question. Because students often need scaffolds as they learn to share ideas in an academic manner, Miss Aitkens provides language frames. After the first read-aloud during which students are answering the text-dependent question, What is this poem about?, Miss Aitkens asks students to talk to partners using this language frame: I think this poem is about _____ because I notice _____. She listens in as Terry and Julie share ideas.

"I think this poem is about things that cover up other things because it talks about blankets covering me up," Terry whispers as Julie listens attentively.

Julie then adds, "I think you're right. I think this poem is about covers because that's the title and it talks about glass and clouds covering."

Satisfied that students are appropriately using the sentence frame to share content ideas, Miss Aitkens moves on to the next read-aloud and asks the text-dependent question: How does the author help you to know what the word *covers* means? After reading, students talk using this language frame: When I see _____, I know that *covers* means _____. Again she listens in as students talk.

Julie starts, "When I see what happens when things get covered, I know that *covers* means they are changed."

Terry, looking a little confused at Julie's statement, adds, "When I see what happens to things that get covered, I know that *covers* means something is laying over something else. Like clouds are over the sky."

Based on this conversation and others in the classroom, Miss Aitkens begins to craft her next question, intended to shed more light on the meaning of *covers*. She continues this lesson, reading aloud, offering text-dependent questions, and providing language frames for student talk.

Miss Aitkens's use of language frames has a twofold benefit. First, it helps focus students on specific, predetermined areas of the text. Second, it provides students with a framework for having scholarly discussions with peers. Eventually a teacher will remove these scaffolds, as students gain more and more automaticity with their use of academic language.

Text Chunking

One reason your students may struggle with the selected text is their inability to manage the entire piece as a whole. For some, it may be difficult to hold onto ideas over the course of the text. Although close reading passages should be short in length, they may be so complex that students have a hard time managing the many ideas they contain. Showing students how to chunk the text into manageable parts can be the scaffold needed to support text comprehension.

Students may naturally chunk the text between paragraphs or lines. For some, however, more chunking may be needed. Show students how drawing lines in the middle of a paragraph and breaking the text into two or more manageable texts might make it less overwhelming. Similarly, students may draw vertical lines through one sentence to break down what each phrase is saying. Notice in the examples in figure 5.7 how each chunk contains a concept. The longer a sentence is, the more concepts it contains. This makes a sentence with many chunks especially complex for all readers, but even more so for those who do not have background knowledge of the topic, those who are not skilled readers, and those who are acquiring English as an additional language.

Grade 1 Example From Mr. Popper's Penguins *(Atwater & Atwater, 1988)*

As he read he could take the little globe that Janie and Bill had given him the Christmas before,|and search out the exact spot he was reading about. (p. 7)

Grade 4 Example From Hurricanes: Earth's Mightiest Storms *(Lauber, 1996)*

Other storms may cover a bigger area|or have higher winds, but|none can match both the size|and the fury of hurricanes. (p. 4)

Grades 6–8 Example From A Short Walk Through the Pyramids and Through the World of Art *(Isaacson, 1993)*

They seem too large to have been made by human beings|, too perfect to have been formed by nature|, and when the sun is overhead|, not solid enough to be attached to the sand. In the minutes before sunrise|, they are the color of faded roses|, and when the last rays of the desert sun touch them, they turn to amber. (pp. 5–7)

Grades 9–10 Example From Circumference: Eratosthenes and the Ancient Quest to Measure the Globe *(Nicastro, 2008)*

This image, which was typically etched on a brass plate|, was inserted into a round frame (the mater)|whose circumference was marked in degrees or hours. (p. 171)

Figure 5.7: Chunking examples.

The following example illustrates using text chunking to support small-group differentiated scaffolding. In Abby Alexander's grade 6 classroom, students are working to decipher complex sentences found in the science text they are reading. Ms. Alexander walks around the room, looking over student work, and notices that two students, Nathaniel and Jackie, are struggling with meaning. She invites them to join her at a corner table and begins to show them how to chunk a complex sentence into more easily digestible parts. She models and thinks aloud for the first sentence.

"I'm looking at this sentence, 'The lava spewed from the volcano, and the ash, greyish and hot, flew from the peak outward to drift over the land.' I know this is complex, with lots of parts, so I'm going to chunk it into simpler parts, which will help me better understand it. My first chunk will be 'The lava spewed from the volcano.' I'm not sure what the word *spewed* means, but I think this chunk of the sentence is saying that lava came out and flowed down. My next chunk says, 'greyish and hot,' which I think means the ash is very hot and it's a grey color. My last chunk says it 'flew from the peak outward to drift over the land.' I think that means the ash is floating over the land before it falls. It's drifting. Now, if I put that all together, I have a picture of lava running down the sides of a volcano and ash floating out of the top. I know the ash is grey and hot. Now I have it! OK. It's your turn to work together to find another complex sentence and chunk it like I did."

Ms. Alexander next lets these two students practice with each other to build their own meaning using chunking.

Think-Alouds

Students may struggle with the ability to think about the main idea and key details. As we noted in chapter 2, they may need an expert (you!) to show them how this sounds and how you go about retrieving information and putting it together. You can use think-alouds in both whole-class and small-group instruction to scaffold learning. Remember to use "I" statements when thinking aloud for students. Once students have observed you doing a think-aloud, you may also have them think aloud about something they are reading. Listening to their thinking about a text gives you insights about how well they are comprehending the text and where they may be having difficulties that need additional scaffolds from you.

The following example illustrates thinking aloud to support small-group differentiated scaffolding. Ms. Sharon Ryan and her fifth graders are reading *Bud, Not Buddy* (Curtis, 1999). She has also been selecting sections to share as close reading passages. After the whole-class close reading, she notices that three students continually have difficulty identifying the main ideas and key details. She decides to have the whole class work on finding details about Flint, Michigan, in 1936 and then compare what they find to life today in their city. As the class works on this activity, she meets with this smaller group to model how she thinks about a short excerpt from the text.

> The woman said, "Now, now, boys, no need to look so glum. I know you don't understand what it means, but there's a depression going on all over this country. People can't find jobs and these are very, very difficult times for everybody. We've been lucky enough to find two wonderful families who've opened their doors for you. I think it's best that we show our new foster families that we're very . . ." (Curtis, 1999, p. 2)

Ms. Ryan provides the following think-aloud for students. She says, "When I read this section, I need to figure out what the text says. I need to pull out the main ideas and some key details in order to get this meaning. Let me reread some of this with that as my focus. I am reading this first sentence and this woman is telling the boys not to be glum. That seems important. I know when people tell young boys something they should listen. But what does *glum* mean? Let me keep reading because I know sometimes authors give hints after the word. This word (pointing to the word) says *depression*. That sounds like *depressed*, and I know what that means. *Glum* probably has something to do with being depressed and the depression going on all over the United States. So a key detail here would be that these boys and maybe the whole country are depressed. That seems pretty important to me. Oh, and if I keep reading I see the word *difficult* and the phrase *can't find jobs*. That would be depressing. When I read on, I see that she has found foster homes for these boys. It really does seem like the main idea is that these boys are glum but that they should be a little less glum because of their new homes. All of these details helped me discover that big or main idea."

Ms. Ryan's thinking aloud provides this small group of students the temporary contingencies they needed to realize what to do when a text initially seems difficult. She illustrates how to use the information she already knows about the vocabulary to support identifying the main idea and key details that are somewhat unclear to her.

Paired Texts

Teachers often stay with the same text to offer instructional contingencies to smaller groups. However, sometimes students need scaffolding that involves using more accessible texts to build the language and background knowledge they need to read the initial text. *Paired texts* are topically related texts, including Internet resources, picture books, documents, magazine or newspaper articles, teacher-created passages, sections from below-grade-level textbooks, readers' theater scripts, and more. When students encounter difficulty with a complex text being used for close reading, paired texts can scaffold student learning. Paired texts introduce vocabulary and concepts through supportive language and illustrations that scaffold comprehension of the close reading text. This does not mean that you *substitute* the more supportive text for the harder one but that you create an instructional contingency that pairs an easier text with your challenging, target text. In this way, teachers help students make connections with topically related ideas and language that will support their greater understanding of the initial complex text. The goal still remains that all students should be reading increasingly complex texts, and to achieve this, they need a lot of instructional scaffolds. A paired text may be one of many scaffolds.

Shanahan (2013) notes:

> Reading multiple texts on a topic written at different levels of difficulty is a terrific scaffold for dealing with harder text. In the past, if a text was hard for students, reading teachers would have encouraged using a different text to be used "instead of." The idea here is not to flee from the hard text, but to read some easier "in addition to" texts on the same topic and to climb these easier texts like stair-steps.

A paired text must not just be easier according to Lexile level but must support identified teaching points. In addition to supporting identified teaching points, paired text sets can (Lapp et al., 2013):

- Promote engagement and build schema for complex concepts
- Provide multiple opportunities for student reading, writing, and speaking and listening to build academic language
- Engage students in synthesizing ideas from multiple texts across one topic
- Build learner capacity for reading increasingly complex texts

To plan for using paired texts, teachers should consider the following five steps (Lapp et al., 2013).

1. Identify the lesson purpose or purposes, appropriate standards, and a short stretch target text for close reading. Analyze the text's complexity and identify teaching points. Create text-dependent questions that ask the reader to look deeply at the text.

2. Select a topically related paired text of increasing difficulty within the grade-appropriate Lexile band that addresses teaching points to support the eventual reading of the complex text.

3. Have students "try on" the more complex text during the large-group close reading. You may have students annotate the text, focusing on important ideas, difficult vocabulary, and confusing areas.

4. Create an instructional contingency lesson around a paired text for students whose performance indicates that they need additional language and content scaffolds.

5. Once they have foundational and language knowledge, return students to the original close reading text and related tasks.

The following example illustrates using paired texts to support small-group differentiated scaffolding. Ms. Celia Young initially selects a complex-text excerpt from *Narrative of the Life of Frederick Douglass, an American Slave, Written by Himself* (Douglass, 2001), a grades 6–8 text exemplar (NGA & CCSSO, n.d.b) for her seventh graders. She plans differentiated scaffolding ahead of time because she knows having background knowledge about the archaic language, author's style, the law, and the racial climate of 1845 will help students grasp the revolutionary nature of the book being published during that time period. For instance, it was illegal to teach slaves how to read and write, and some white people had deeply held beliefs about black people being inferior. At the conclusion of the whole-class close reading, she realizes there are five students who aren't able to capture the text's main ideas and details because they do not have a basic understanding of this period of history or the skills needed to read the text. She asks these students to work with her in a smaller group, focusing on a topically related paired text to build the information and required skills needed to analyze the more complex text.

At this point, Ms. Young introduces and reads aloud the picture book *Words Set Me Free: The Story of Young Frederick Douglass* (Cline-Ransome, 2012), which portrays the central role that literacy played in Douglass's life. It recounts how his owner's wife illicitly taught him the letters of the alphabet and the dangers associated with this act. It ends with a cliff-hanger, briefly detailing Douglass's first failed attempt to escape the South. Because it follows the outlines of the original close reading text but stops at a strategic point, it will spark students' interest (Moss, 2012).

With its clear message and explanations, this picture book biography provides the background knowledge these students need to appreciate the original close reading text. It positions these students to resume their close reading of the original Douglass memoir armed with the knowledge they need to re-encounter the text in a meaningful way. Note that Ms. Young does not simply give students an easier book to read; she scaffolds their reading of a complex text with an easier one, but then takes them right back to the challenging text. After reading this paired text, the five students and Ms. Young return to the original text. Ms. Young asks them to reread the passage to see if they can share what basic right Frederick Douglass believed everyone should have. When Keisha quickly shares that Douglass wanted to have the right to read and learn, and Blair adds, "Yes and he wasn't getting to learn how because he was a slave," Ms. Young asks the students to further share the details in the passage that supported their thinking. Jayden notes that in paragraph one Douglass "always took his bread with him to give to the poorer white kids as a trade for teaching him to read." Since it is now clear these students have the gist or literal understanding of the text, Ms. Young moves to questions about the language in the text that helped them to more deeply realize the suffering Douglass experienced. Once she is sure that they also realize the connection Douglass is making between reading and freedom, she has these five students join the class, which is working in pairs to practice orally sharing Douglass's speech.

Through this type of scaffolding, Ms. Young modeled for these students what to do when they find a text too difficult. Ms. Young's actions taught these students to not give up but rather to self-monitor to determine why they were not succeeding and then move to a less difficult text to build the skills and knowledge that enable them to return to the initially complex text. Always consider the individual reader and his or her skills and knowledge as you determine each text-complexity feature.

Conclusion

Being able to deeply analyze what a text says involves an interaction between the reader and the text. The depth of that interaction is dependent on the reader having a basic understanding of the language the author uses to convey the information or tell the story and also on his or her base of existing knowledge about the topic being shared in the text. Additionally the reader's skill in knowing how to employ these bases of knowledge to deeply analyze what the text says is foundational when reading complex texts. The question becomes, What happens when a student is asked to closely read a grade level or above complex text and experiences limited success because he or she does not have the necessary language, base of knowledge, or reading skills? The student's success becomes dependent on a skilled teacher who designs instructional scaffolds. The scenarios shared in this chapter offer examples of teachers scaffolding instruction that supports students in developing the language, skills, and knowledge to support their understanding of what the text says.

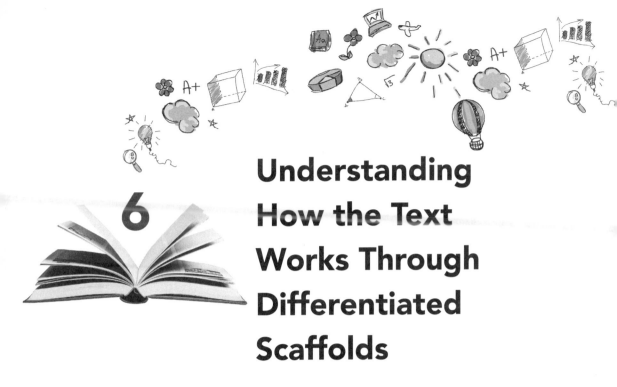

6 Understanding How the Text Works Through Differentiated Scaffolds

Virginia Woolf (1925) writes of fellow novelist Joseph Conrad, ". . . the vision of a novelist is both complex and specialized" (p. 225). The same can be said for the op-ed writer supporting her argument with research-based evidence, the historian who documents noted events within a social context, and for the poet who conveys sentiments in lyrical verse. The written word can be laid down in a variety of ways, some of which follow the particular rules and expectations of a certain genre or area of publication, while incorporating both academic and technical words and phrases. Complexity is at the heart of such writing—in quantity, quality, and in relation to the skills and experiences the reader brings to the text.

Students as young as third grade are expected to recognize the relationships these text structures convey. Most teachers, however, will agree that in virtually every class there are students who struggle with these complex conventions of language. Comprehension increases greatly when text structures are accurately identified and interpreted. Given this, a prepared educator who plans well will have contingencies on hand to support learners who need extra scaffolds to support them identifying text structures and their impact on the meaning of the text.

This chapter examines five areas of instruction that can be implemented as scaffolds to support students recognizing or using structure to negotiate meaning within an informational or narrative text: (1) recognition of signal words, (2) multimedia supports, (3) intense vocabulary instruction, (4) think-alouds for pictures, charts, and graphs, and (5) text-dependent layered questions. Both informational and narrative texts are often jam-packed with clues to meaning, identified or understood by a close examination of the text's workings. Many readers are unaware or inexperienced at noticing such clues and often miss them or overlook their meaning.

Recognition of Signal Words

Writers and speakers guide their audiences with words and phrases that indicate relationships and connections among ideas. Words like *first, next, finally, similarly, unlike,* and *however* and phrases like *in contrast, moving on, to begin with,* and *having considered* are referred to as *signal words* because they help signal the direction of the author's thinking. The following scenario from Lena Toussaint's third-grade classroom illustrates how differentiated scaffolding around identification of signal words supports a small group of students.

Students are addressing the Next Generation Science Standard 3-LS4-1 (NGSS Lead States, 2013): "Analyze and interpret data from fossils to provide evidence of the organisms and the environments in which they lived long ago." Miss Toussaint decides to conduct a close reading of text exemplar *Boy, Were We Wrong About Dinosaurs!* (Kudlinski, 2005) from appendix B of the Common Core State Standards (NGA & CCSSO, n.d.b). She often uses close reading to guide her students to address science standards. Her instruction blends both English language arts and science content. This particular lesson involves a whole-class close reading, subsequent differentiated scaffolding for students needing additional supports, and a final project that provides students an opportunity to apply their new understandings.

Miss Toussaint gives students copies of the exemplar. Students number sentences so they can easily refer to them when engaged in peer and whole-class conversations. Next, she asks students to read through the text while thinking about her first text-dependent question, What is this passage about? She reminds students to use information from the text to support their responses. Once students finish the first reading that involves annotating the text, they engage in partner talk to share their initial understandings of the text.

David's partner, Juan, says he thinks the text is about "the mistakes people make when looking at dinosaur bones."

"How do you know this?" asks David.

Juan responds, "It says something about Iguanodon in lines seven through thirteen, but I got confused about what was before and what is today."

David adds, "Yeah, it says it in sentence eight, 'our own past guesses about dinosaurs were as wrong as those about ancient China' [NGA & CCSSO, n.d.b, p. 56]. I get that some of our past guesses were wrong, but I don't get the China part."

Miss Toussaint, makes a note on her note-taking chart (figures 4.1 and 4.2, pages 73 and 74) that these two boys may need to work with her in a smaller group after the whole-group instruction. She specifically identifies that both need to understand how the chunks fit together in order to get a clear understanding of a text. On her clipboard she writes, "Understand how signal words support whole-text comprehension. May need to meet with students who need more work seeing relationships presented throughout a text. Prepare differentiated scaffolds."

Additionally, Miss Toussaint recognizes that being able to read this descriptive passage and create a mental time line is appropriate because often in scientific and historical readings authors identify past errors in investigations as a means of comparison with new research and data. Miss Toussaint knows that if students are able to focus on key signal words that indicate relationships between information contained throughout the text, they are better able to analyze scientific and historical texts.

Because David, Juan, and a few other students seem confused about signal words, Miss Toussaint asks her next question, which she plans on the spot as a result of this observation, What words does the author use to signal to us that our knowledge about dinosaurs has changed over time? Again the students return to the text to find the exact signal words the author uses to support their understanding that the structure of this passage is descriptive. The conversation that results provides most of the students the support they need to continue with the passage, but Miss Toussaint again notes that she needs to provide David and Juan additional instruction on signal words because they did not see the connection between signal words and the changes in scientists' understanding about dinosaurs.

Before she provides differentiated scaffolds for these students, she presents a group project related to the reading for the whole class to complete—a collaborative poster. She asks the whole class to meet in teams of four to first talk about content, come to consensus regarding what had been shared, and collaborate to create a poster illustrating how people have been wrong about dinosaurs. She tasks each group with creating a then-and-now time frame poster that shows the old view of a dinosaur alongside the current view using words from the text and also their drawings, based on their interpretations of the text as a group. While most of the class starts on this, Miss Toussaint meets with David and Juan, who need differentiated scaffolds to support their understanding of the structural pattern of this text by working with signal words.

Miss Toussaint provides David and Juan with a chart (table 6.1, page 110) that contains text-structure terms related to the dinosaur text and other texts students would be reading soon. Miss Toussaint wants them to focus on only a few words at a time so as not to become overwhelmed. Additionally, she wants them to become familiar with the kinds of text-structure terms they would likely encounter in their current texts—those appropriate for third graders. In the future, Miss Toussaint intends to build on this text-structure lesson by adding more terms to students' repertoires of relationship language. She wants to avoid later confusion for the entire class.

Table 6.1: Text-Structure Signal Words

Relationships Between Words and Phrases	Signal Words	Examples
Sequence: Shows order	*first, next, then, last, now, later* *ago, when, then*	First, we collected bones. Later we noticed that they were from a dinosaur. Now we are going to find out what kind of dinosaur had these bones.
Description: Connects to characteristics or examples of a topic, person, place, thing, or idea	*for example, such as, like, as*	These dinosaurs walked on four legs, like a dog.
Compare and contrast: Shows how two or more things are similar or how they are different	*in comparison, on the one hand, but on the other hand*	In comparison to the dinosaur bones, the bird bones were very small.
Problem and solution: Shows a problem and an answer or way to solve the problem	*the question is, to solve this, one suggestion, an answer is*	To solve the mystery of dinosaur size, the scientists used computer modeling.

To share with David and Juan how they might use this chart to identify signal words and make meaning, Miss Toussaint models her own thinking about these terms using another text. Let's look at Miss Toussaint's think-aloud.

"I'm going to read a part of this text about polar bears (Thomson, 2010). You can look on your copy and follow along.

> When the cub was born four months ago, he was no bigger than a guinea pig. Blind and helpless, he snuggled in his mother's fur. He drank her milk and grew, safe from the long Arctic winter. Outside the den, on some days, it was fifty degrees below zero. From October to February, the sun never rose. Now it is spring—even though snow still covers the land. The cub is about the size of a cocker spaniel. He's ready to leave the den. For the first time, he sees bright sunlight and feels the wind ruffle his fur. [NGA & CCSSO, n.d.b, p. 57]

"Just like the text about dinosaurs, this text has signal words that can help us learn more about the meaning. I'm going to use my chart to find those words. Let's see if you can find the same ones. I see the words *when* and *ago* in the first sentence. Do you see that?

My chart tells me these are sequence words. I'm going to reread that sentence. 'When the cub was born four months ago, he was no bigger than a guinea pig' [p. 57].

"I can tell that this was a while ago. Time has passed. I'm going to find another signal word. There's a sentence that uses *now*. It says, 'Now it's spring' [p. 57].

"This is also a sequence word. I can tell that we are talking about how it is in the present time, today. This text has me moving forward in time as it tells me the story of the polar bear cub. My chart says that sequence words tell the order of events. If it's spring now, it must have been winter when the cub was born four months ago. It does mention winter. Do you see how you can use this chart to help you see how words are connected? Now it's your turn to try this. Go back to the text and work with a partner to find text structure words on our chart. Then, see if you can find meaning."

David and Juan are quickly able to identify words such as *when* and *like a*, noting that the first indicated time, and the second was a description term. Both students unlock new meaning and seem confident in their understanding of the identification of key words as a way to identify the structure of a text. After one final rereading of the initial text, David and Juan join two other students to create a group of four to work on their collaborative poster.

Multimedia Supports

Complex texts have organizational structures that are intricate. They may combine multiple structures or genres in an abstract manner. Readers might encounter several theses and may see in some texts sophisticated organization appropriate for a particular discipline. For instance, a primary historical source document may have a preamble or articles. A science text might have an abstract or a data-analysis section. Teachers often offer readers multimedia materials such as visuals—photos and artifacts, transcriptions of a text, and video—as scaffolds to support their comprehension. In the following example, consider how Miss Toussaint uses multimedia supports to provide differentiated instruction for students who struggle with comprehending text organization.

During Miss Toussaint's formative assessment of the whole-class close reading of *Boy, Were We Wrong About Dinosaurs!* (Kudlinski, 2005), she notes on her note-taking chart that in addition to David and Juan (see "Recognition of Signal Words" in this chapter), she needs to give extra support to two other students, Chad and Demetria, who have difficulty understanding how the text is organized. Once the whole class begins a group poster activity, Miss Toussaint prepares to conduct differentiated scaffolding for Chad and Demetria. She doesn't call Chad and Demetria by name but just touches their backs and invites them to join her. She tells David and Juan, who are working with them on their group poster, that they will be back in a few minutes to finish the poster work.

Sharing a copy of the dinosaur text with Chad and Demetria, she says, "Let's look at this text for a moment. There's a paragraph near the end that seems to have caught your attention. Let's think about the words the author uses to signal to us that our thinking changed over time.

> Some of our first drawings of dinosaurs showed them with their elbows and knees pointing out to the side, like a lizard's. With legs like that, big dinosaurs could only waddle clumsily on all fours or float underwater. Now we know that their legs were straight under them, like a horse's. Dinosaurs were not clumsy. The sizes and shapes of their leg bones seem to show that some were as fast and graceful as deer. (NGA & CCSSO, n.d.b, p. 56)

"Now let's consider this question: What words does the author use to signal to us that our knowledge about dinosaurs has changed over time? The question is asking about how scientists think about the past. I have some websites and a video I want you to watch."

Miss Toussaint next shares a photo of an ammonite fossil from a website (Aquarium of the Pacific, n.d.a). She notes, "These organisms have been studied by scientists. If you first looked at the photo of the ammonite, what might you think about its movement in the ocean?"

Chad replies, "It looks heavy, like it would sink."

"Now let's look at a relative, or family member, of an ammonite. This is a nautilus." Miss Toussaint clicks on the nautilus link to share the image (Aquarium of the Pacific, n.d.b). "What do you think of this creature? How might it move through the ocean?"

Chad notices the tentacles coming out of the shell. "Maybe it moves those to swim," he states.

Next Miss Toussaint shares a short video clip that shows how we understand the past by looking at layers of rock and fossils in the Grand Canyon (NOVA, n.d.). While Miss Toussaint understands that students can use signal words to identify sequences of time, she also knows that they can benefit from understanding how signal words connect to content in the real world. To guide students toward this understanding, she shares the video so that students see how time sequences connect to changes in organisms within the discipline of science. Clarifying the connections she was trying to make, Miss Toussaint shares, "At the end of the video, you saw a chambered nautilus. You saw how it moved through the ocean in the video. When you first looked at the ammonite fossil I shared, would you have guessed that a similar relative could move so smoothly through the ocean?"

In unison, the students shout, "No!" Chad adds, "In the video, it moved easily through the water. Maybe the ammonite moved like that, too."

Miss Toussaint says, "You just revised your idea about how the ammonite and nautilus move, like scientists do. Now let's go back to the text and think about the question I asked before, What words does the author use to signal to us that our knowledge about dinosaurs has changed over time? How does the author describe changes?"

Chad and Demetria review the text. Then Demetria notes, "I think the first drawings of a dinosaur were wrong. They had elbows and knees pointing to the side. This line says, 'Now we know that their legs were straight under them, like a horse's' [NGA & CCSSO, p. 56]. Line 17 tells how scientists change their ideas when they learn new things."

Chad adds, "Yes, now I get it. And there are other examples here, too. Like this part in sentence eleven about the spike on Iguanodon. It was on his hands, not his nose like they first thought." Satisfied that students are starting to delve more deeply into the text, making logical connections, and more readily able to navigate the complexities, Miss Toussaint asks these two students to join the rest of the class and to continue working on their poster team.

The differentiated scaffolding took about ten minutes to implement. It was intentionally short and focused to ensure that Chad and Demetria would get the support they needed and would also be able to rejoin the whole class to engage in the poster activity. After the posters are complete, group members sign their name on the back using their own colored marker. This helps Ms. Toussaint identify the contributions each student makes.

Through attentive formative assessment, Miss Toussaint identifies the students' instructional needs and then moves these students toward deeper understandings of foundational concepts in science and toward more profound understandings of language used in the text.

Intense Vocabulary Instruction

Sometimes the challenging part of determining how the text works comes from understanding the vocabulary. As we've noted, often the vocabulary, especially of informational text that is highly academic, subject specific, demanding, nuanced, and context dependent can be difficult for some readers. Let's see how Toby Stowell, tenth-grade history teacher, supports students who at the end of a close reading still need differentiated scaffolds focused on vocabulary to help their deep understanding of the text.

Together the class has been reading *Bury My Heart at Wounded Knee: An Indian History of the American West* (Brown, 1970). Mr. Stowell reads part of chapter 1 as a shared reading. Then, he asks students to read and annotate an excerpt of chapter 1 that is also included in appendix B of the CCSS (NGA & CCSSO, n.d.b). After students number the passage into seven chunks, Mr. Stowell says, "Read your numbered text and think about the question, What is this passage about? Be sure to consider the groups who were involved." Mr. Stowell observes students as they read and annotate on the text. He notes on the note-taking guide on his clipboard (figure 4.1, page 73) that a few students are boxing words and phrases and adding question marks beside them. After partner conversation about the general meaning of the text, he asks what the phrase *blotted out* means in the first chunk, "The great Cherokee nation had survived more than a hundred years of the white man's wars, diseases, and whiskey, but now it was to be blotted out" [NGA & CCSSO, n.d.b, p. 130].

D'Angelo replies, "It means to be destroyed."

"How did you figure that out?" Mr. Stowell asks.

"My clue came from the words *but now* in chunk number one," D'Angelo says.

"Wonderful reading; you noticed the signal words! As we discussed last week, it is so important to pay close attention to the clues the author puts in sentences to help us get the meaning of words that we don't know or ones that are used in different ways," responds Mr. Stowell, reinforcing the signal words strategy students had learned previously.

After additional conversation about the passage, Mr. Stowell continues reading the remainder of the chapter aloud. He notes from the conversations that occurred during the close reading and subsequent shared reading that six students still need additional support to help them develop a strategy for understanding complex language that interferes with their comprehension. Before beginning his contingency instruction with the small group that needs support, Mr. Stowell provides the whole class with a task. He explains, "I'd like you to work with your table partner to write a minimum of five sentences that summarize the main points of the section of the text we have just read. You should use at least three sentence frames from our list of sentence frames on the board." (See figure 6.1 for the sentence frames Mr. Stowell provides.)

- According to the text _____.
- Based on what the author states, I determine that _____.
- The author describes _____.
- I determined that _____.
- To conclude _____.
- First _____. Following this, _____. Finally, _____.
- The author points out _____.

Figure 6.1: Sentence frame examples.

Mr. Stowell then taps the shoulders of the six students he wants to meet with for contingency instruction. Together they move to a round table on the side of the classroom. Here's how Mr. Stowell offers a differentiated scaffold to support these students understanding the vocabulary they were finding perplexing.

"There are lots of new and challenging words in this text. Let's examine some of them in greater depth. I have a chart here. This is called a *vocabulary self-awareness chart*. It's blank now, but let's put our challenging words on the chart. I'll start the list. I want to add the word *frontier*. Jahlil, what words do you think are challenging?"

Jahlil responds, "We have to add *clamor*."

Before Jahlil is able to offer another term, Jennifer jumps in, nearly shouting, "*Exodus*. That word is holding me back. The only time I ever heard that was in a song, and I didn't know what it meant then. Put that one down." Other students continue to add words until the list comprises eight words (figure 6.2).

Mr. Stowell begins to model. "I want you each to go through this list. I know that many of these are unfamiliar words, but these are all words we will learn if you don't know them already. And I think that some of you might know a little about these words. Here's what I would like you to do now. If you can give both a *definition* of the term and an *example* of the term, put an X in the first column that has a plus (+) sign. Then write the definition and the example in the appropriate boxes. If you can give just one, a definition or an example, put an X in the check mark (✓) column. Then write what you know in the corresponding column. If you don't know either, a definition or an example, it's OK. Just put an X in the minus sign (–) column. Let me model first—I'm going to focus on the word *frontier*. I think that an example of a *frontier* is a place where the Cherokee were sent. I think this because it says in the text, 'Scarcely were the refugees settled behind the security of the permanent Indian frontier when soldiers began marching westward through Indian country' [NGA & CCSSO, n.d.b, p. 130]. The word *settled* makes me think of a place where people go to live. Remember when we talked about the early settlers? Also, the sentence mentions *Indian country*. I think this is where they lived. Even though I can give an example of *frontier*—where the Indians went to live—I really don't know a clear definition. I'm going to put an X in the check mark column. Now it's your turn. Use the text and your own background knowledge to complete the chart."

Word	+ Can provide definition & example	✓ Can provide definition or example	– Cannot provide definition or example	Definition	Example
frontier					
clamor					
exodus					
trek					
remnants					
scarcely					
refugees					
expanse					

Figure 6.2: Semantic feature-analysis chart.

The students work to complete the chart. Some know definitions and others can provide examples. The vocabulary knowledge is variable. A few words are completely unknown to all students. After working together as a small group, all students have an increased understanding of the vocabulary. Mr. Stowell invites this group to join the rest of the class to finish their summary writing. Knowing that vocabulary knowledge is critical to understanding this particular text, Mr. Stowell decides to offer deeper vocabulary instruction to all students after they have completed their summary writing task.

"I'm going to give everyone five index cards. I'd like to challenge you to find up to five words that are confusing you or you are uncertain about. Some of you may find only three or four. That's OK. Write these words on the front of your index card." Mr. Stowell then provides a notebook ring for each student and asks them to punch holes in the corners of their cards so that they hang on the ring. "Now you may use your online dictionaries to identify definitions for these words," he tells them. He then offers a challenge, "When we finish, I want you to share your definitions with three adults in your life—another teacher, a parent, an older sibling, grandparent, uncle, neighbor, or anyone else. Ask each adult to sign the back of the last blank card. Then bring it back in to class for credit."

Mr. Stowell also directs students to notice when they hear these words in class. Toward the end of the unit, he even has Jahlil, Jennifer, and the rest of the small group that received the differentiated scaffold go back to the vocabulary self-awareness chart to clarify areas that they were previously confused about and add missing definitions and examples.

Through the intense vocabulary instruction, Mr. Stowell focused students on their own identified list of roadblock words. He worked with students to heighten awareness of the meanings and suggested that students listen for when the words are used in class. Consequently, students began to pay attention to and understand the context for using the words. This contingency instruction is well worth the time when vocabulary is a roadblock.

Think-Alouds for Pictures, Charts, and Graphs

Some students find the interpretation of *visual supports* and *layout* challenging to inter-pret. Text placement that includes columns or very small fonts can be difficult. Text features like intricate charts, graphs, photos, tables and diagrams, and headings and subheadings may require inferencing skills and being able to synthesize information. As we've noted in chapter 5 (page 85), think-alouds are a great way for teachers to support students as they attempt to understand difficult written texts. They can also be imple-mented with these complex visual aspects of texts.

Let's visit Coni Verdugo's fifth-grade classroom to consider reader and task concerns, using a classroom example related to an informational science text: *Next Time You See a Maple Seed* (Morgan, 2014). Ms. Verdugo knows that this text might be challenging for some students because of the scarcity of maple trees in Southern California where they live. To motivate students for this reading, she decides to engage them in a community service task and a related writing experience before beginning a close reading of the text.

With her principal's support, Ms. Verdugo organizes a tree-planting event at her school site. The class plants five trees—varieties indigenous to the locale—on Arbor Day. Additionally, Ms. Verdugo bookmarks two websites on the student tablets—one that allows the fifth graders to examine the characteristics of the sugar maple and the other that looks at red maple trees (Cornell Sugar Maple Research and Extension Program, n.d.b, n.d.c).

These experiences provide a context for accomplishing the lesson purpose of understanding plants and their structures. The following week as they read *Next Time You See a Maple Seed*, Ms. Verdugo invites students to closely read sections to guide them as they deeply examine the text. She crafts specific text-dependent questions to direct students to aspects of the photos that appear in the book and to derive word meaning through inference, text clues, and a look at text structure. Partner talk and note taking in Foldables are also key elements of this text examination.

Before beginning the first reading, students make their Foldables (figure 6.3) containing sections addressing three prompts: (1) What big ideas does this book share?, (2) What details does the author provide to help clarify sunlight's role in a maple tree's growth and survival?, and (3) How does the author let you know the chronological order of events in her descriptions of the maple tree's growth? Why did the author include the photo on page 19? The Foldable serves as a note-taking chart. Because it is organized into three sections, the students are able to identify big ideas or the general understanding of the information and note it under flap one. Students note the key details and chronology of how a maple tree begins and grows under flap two. By doing so they refine their general understandings while considering why the author shared specific information and pictures. They then note these final insights under flap three. Noting all of this information helps them understand the work and message of the author.

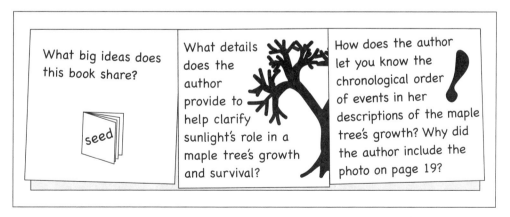

Figure 6.3: Foldable example.

As Ms. Verdugo listens in on partner talk following each reading, she notices that four students need extra support. These students seem to understand structure, notice details to clarify the role of sunlight in plant growth, and identify chronological order of events noted in the text, but they struggle with the concepts connected to the photo showing a young plant with the wing of the samara still attached. They struggle with interpreting the visual supports provided in the text. Ms. Verdugo wonders if these students are unable to grasp the ideas related to the fruit developing into a plant. She wants them to understand how the samara, with its embryo, forms a plant. To help with this, Ms. Verdugo decides that she needs to work with them while the other students begin their extension of the new information they learned. Before we look at the differentiated scaffold she offers this smaller group, let's look at the extension task that involves the other students writing in response to one of several RAFT writing prompts she shared. To view a video of a class engaging in RAFT writing, visit http://www.learner.org/courses/readwrite/video-detail /power-writing-science.html. This video is part of the series *Reading & Writing in the Disciplines*, which can be accessed on the Annenberg Learner website at www.learner.org.

Ms. Verdugo offers the following RAFTs and asks the students to select the one they prefer (figure 6.4).

Option 1	Option 2
Role: Maple seed	**R**ole: Samara of a maple tree
Audience: Child who will plant the seed	**A**udience: The wind
Format: Cartoon	**F**ormat: Email
Topic: What I need to grow	**T**opic: My journey to become a tree

Figure 6.4: RAFT options.

She also gives them the option of creating their own RAFTs with her approval. These RAFT-writing experiences help Ms. Verdugo's students summarize and organize their thinking after reading the text. It is a strategic task that guides them to clarify ideas in written form while allowing the teacher to assess their comprehension of the text. Additionally, as students work on their RAFT assignments, Ms. Verdugo has time to work with the smaller group of students who need a differentiated scaffold to support their deep analysis of the text.

While the members of the larger group work on their RAFTs, Ms. Verdugo and the smaller group work together before rejoining them for this assignment. Lamar, one of the four students working with Ms. Verdugo, has noted at the end of the whole-class close reading that he is confused about what "the samara was all about." Ms. Verdugo asks Lamar and the three others to listen as she thinks out loud about a diagram from a website that helps clarify the samara's role (Cornell Sugar Maple Research and Extension Program, n.d.a).

She begins, "I can see from the photo that the seed is produced by pollination. We learned about that last week. The seed in the diagram looks just like the ones in the book we just read. There are two wings on this seed. Now I'm noticing that the seed has an arrow next to it that is pointing to the seedling. The seedling looks like a little plant. I think this means that the seed is going to develop into a baby plant that will grow to become a big tree."

In this vein, Ms. Verdugo continues her think-aloud for another two minutes. She wants to demonstrate the metacognitive processes that come into play when considering a visual like a diagram or a photo. After the think-aloud, Ms. Verdugo asks the four students to reread the original text and think aloud in whisper voices with a partner about a photo in the text. Listening to their whispering allows for further assessment.

Lamar whispers: "I see part of the feather part of the samara. And there's a leaf coming out of it. I wonder if that is showing that the plant grows from the seed. It's almost like it's breaking out of the seed. That's so cool!"

Jack, another group member, whispers: "I see that leaf coming out of the seed, too. I wonder if that little plant started as that seed when it was in the ground. Maybe the little tree came from the seed in the ground and grew up, out of the ground."

As she listens to each student's whispered think-aloud, she is confident that he or she can now negotiate and clarify the text's meaning by inferring and synthesizing information from a visual support. Additionally, these students are developing the metacognitive skills required to glean information from closely reading a text with pictures, charts, and graphs.

Text-Dependent Layered Questions

As mentioned in early chapters, the use of text-dependent layered questions can be an effective strategy for supporting both small groups and whole classes as students grapple with text meaning. The following scenario features instruction for the whole class rather than differentiated or contingency scaffolding for a small group. We have included this to emphasize that once teachers write and ask the initial questions, they may find that many students are not able to analyze the text's meaning. It would then be very appropriate to ask additional layered questions to support the entire class. When students are investigating the workings of the text—specifically vocabulary, craft, and style—a teacher might have a series of layered questions ready to use when needed. If, for example, students don't respond with understanding to a question about the author's craft, a teacher could offer a next question strategically intended to focus the students on an aspect of the text that would unlock meaning about this area of difficulty. Teachers should listen very carefully to their students' responses, as they will indicate the depth of layering that is needed. It's important that teachers have read the text very closely and considered where their students may need them to layer questions. This type of preparation affords you the opportunity to have layered questions ready.

The following example illustrates using layered questions to support small-group differentiated scaffolding. Mr. Don West's sixth graders are reading Nikki Giovanni's (2007) poem, "A Poem for My Librarian, Mrs. Long." Mr. West begins with a general understanding question that asks students, What's this poem about? After listening in on partner talk, he is satisfied that students understand that it is about a little girl thanking her librarian for getting her books to read. Next, to engage students in thinking about how the text works, Mr. West asks students, "Why does the author use a writing style that doesn't always follow the rules of grammar?"

Listening in on student talk, Mr. West assesses his students' understanding of author's style only to conclude that many cannot even speculate about an answer to this question.

One student, Todd, tells his partner Shannon, "I don't know why she would write this way. We could get a bad grade for something like this."

Shannon replies, "Maybe the author didn't like school, and this is just her style 'cause she didn't learn it."

Given the need for further investigation of author's style, Mr. West decides to read the poem aloud so the students can hear a fluent reading of the poem. He believes this will support their comprehension. He reads the first verse and asks students to listen and read along and then annotate in response to the layered question, Do you think the author wanted a particular sound? Explain your thinking.

Following the shared reading, Mr. West again asks students to use their annotations to talk about the text. He notes some hesitation in their responses and asks the entire class, "How does the poem sound?"

Mario responds, "It sounds like a song. It's easy to hear."

Mr. West then asks, "Do you think the author wanted a particular sound? Explain your thinking."

Mario replies, "I think the author wanted it to sound like this. She loved to read, and her poem sounds like a song."

Karina agrees, "Yes, it makes me picture a little girl and how she might have felt getting books to read. It sounds more real and musical, like you said, Mario. I guess it's OK to break some rules in grammar. Maybe the author did this to give a feeling."

Mr. West knows that listening to student talk reveals whether they understand the workings of the text. He is prepared to provide layered questions in case students are unable to respond to the initial more complex question. Recall that after the first general understanding question, Mr. West asked students, "Why does the author use a writing style that doesn't always follow the rules of grammar?" By listening in on partner talk, he realizes that students need another question, a layered question, to help them delve deeper. He asks them to listen as he reads the poem so that they can address the question, How does the poem sound? Do you think the author wanted a particular sound? Explain your thinking. In this example, Mr. West's layered questions strategically lead students to a better understanding of the author's style. If these layered questions had not moved all students in the class to a deep understanding of this text, Mr. West would now have begun working with smaller groups and providing the contingency scaffolds he had assessed were needed.

Guiding students to understand the workings of the text takes time, but the payoff is large. In particular, when students are working to find deep meaning by reading and rereading complex texts that hold nuanced and subtle clues to comprehension, scaffolded instruction propelled by layered questioning may provide just the tools needed to unlock hidden meanings for students who initially struggle with the text. Developing proficiency in interpreting the text's workings leads students toward more independent mastery of reading, especially when it comes to complex texts.

Conclusion

Providing the particular support needed to help students understand the intricacies of a text is clearly challenging. Ongoing formative assessment is the best way for teachers to identify the specific needs that students have when trying to negotiate meaning. When students struggle with text organization, visual supports and layout, relationships among ideas, or with vocabulary, meaningful scaffolds guide students from confusion to clarified comprehension.

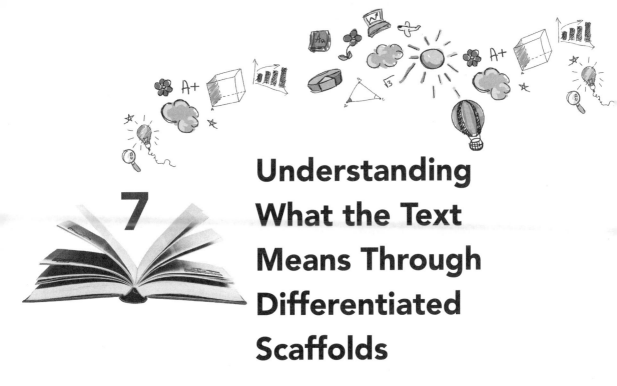

7 Understanding What the Text Means Through Differentiated Scaffolds

Without a clear understanding of the language the author uses to convey meaning, readers are often unable to make inferences because they do not glean clues while reading. This prevents them from putting the pieces together that would help them deeply understand the author's purpose, bias, intentions, or the interconnections of ideas within the text and also as it relates to other texts on the same topic.

While the author's vocabulary and language use are certainly dimensions of every facet of comprehension, we emphasize language as a primary feature of understanding what a text means because it is well known among educators that the level of one's understanding of language either aids or hinders literacy learning (Dickinson & Tabors, 2001; Snow, Burns, & Griffin, 1998). Therefore, the instruction shared in this chapter focuses on familiar routines that can serve as differentiated scaffolds to support students making meaning of a complex text by deeply analyzing the author's use of language: (1) text-dependent questions, (2) think-alouds with annotation, (3) graphic organizers, (4) visual text, (5) word sorts, and (6) word work.

Text-Dependent Questions

Text-dependent questions are very helpful as a scaffold for students who struggle with the language of a text. With a careful diagnosis, teachers can ask the perfect question at the perfect time in order for students to be successful meaning makers. While text-dependent questions can be part of everyday instruction for ensuring student understanding of what a text means, some students need to be asked additional questions as differentiated scaffolds to help them understand the various aspects of a text's deeper meaning. When selecting a group of students or individuals to work explicitly with these dimensions of language, the questions in table 7.1 may be helpful in focusing your instruction.

Table 7.1: Possible Questions for Facilitating Understanding of a Text's Meaning

Language Consideration	Possible Questions
Author's Style and Tone	• What words are unfamiliar to you? Can the surrounding words help you with the meaning of the unknown word? • What is the author's attitude about what is going on? What words tell you the attitude?
Author's Purpose	• The author wrote this text for a very deliberate reason. What words or phrases tell you why the author wrote this text? • Think of why authors write. Do you see words that entertain you, give you information, or persuade you?
Theme	• What is the underlying message or big idea of this text? How do you know? • Look for words, phrases, or ideas that repeat. How do those help you understand the text's theme?
Point of View	• What is the point of view? How do you know? • Look carefully at the words the author uses. How do the pronouns help you understand the point of view? How do proper nouns help you?
Use of Language	• Is this word being compared to something else? (metaphor and simile) Why would the author make this comparison? • Are there any words that have the same sound, for example the /m/ sound? (alliteration) Why would the author use these similar sounding words? • Where does the author give human qualities to an animal, object, or idea? (personification) Why would the author do this? • Did the author use any words or phrases to appeal to your senses? (imagery) Why would an author do this?
Language Register	• What might you say in this situation? How does that sound similar to what this other character said? • Do any of the words in this text look like words you know in English?

The following example illustrates asking text-dependent questions to support small-group differentiated scaffolding for understanding what the text means. As seventh-grade

English teacher Elana Kennedy mingles among her students as they engage in a close reading of "Thank You, M'am" by Langston Hughes, she uses the rubric from figure 4.1 (page 73) to record information about the students' behaviors that will help her evaluate how well each understands the text. She notes that, as students annotate, many are circling words and adding question marks next to phrases. In most cases, students are writing in the margins about what they think the words mean. Being the effective teacher she is, Ms. Kennedy asks text-dependent questions and engages students in collaborative conversations about the text and their annotations.

At the conclusion of the close reading, most students have accomplished the lesson purpose by understanding the text well enough to infer that its deepest meaning conveys the idea that acts of kindness can positively impact others. However, there are still three students who do not understand the meaning of the text because of the unfamiliarity of the language, which is too much of a stretch for them without some scaffolding. Ms. Kennedy knows that this small group needs to meet with her to analyze the language of the text as a way to develop an understanding of the author's language choices, style and tone, purpose, theme, and point of view. Her goal is to teach them to use context whenever possible to understand unfamiliar language. Before beginning work with this small group, Ms. Kennedy asks the other students to use the text to first identify how, in the story, Roger is changed by Mrs. Jones's treatment of him. She asks them to note several pieces of evidence that show how the change in Roger occurs gradually and then to share their thinking by writing a letter to Mrs. Jones from Roger as an adult, describing how she changed his life.

As the larger group begins to work, Ms. Kennedy meets with Rita, Davion, and Diamond to look a little more closely at some of the words and phrases that seem to be interfering with their comprehension. The following conversation illustrates how her questioning achieves the instructional purpose of helping this small group of students learn to use context to unlock the meanings of words, which will ultimately help them to better understand the deeper message of the text.

Targeting the word *frail*, which these students earlier circled and identified as not understanding, Ms. Kennedy says, "Let's look at the text again and see if we can figure out how Roger ends up in this situation."

Rita explains, "Roger fell when he tried to grab Mrs. Jones's purse."

Ms. Kennedy responds, "Yes. And, from the text, can you see what caused this? See if you can picture this in your mind."

Diamond notes, "It says in paragraph one that he lost his balance."

"What caused this?" Ms. Kennedy asks.

Davion adds, "It also says in paragraph one that, 'the weight of the purse and the boy's weight caused him to lose his balance.'"

Diamond says, "So he was big and thought the purse was going to be heavy, but it wasn't."

Rita responds, "In chunk 15 it says he was 'frail,' so maybe *frail* means he wasn't big and the purse was heavy."

Davion adds, "Yes, so it probably knocked him over."

Diamond responds, "Oh I see. The heavy purse made him fall because it weighed more than him."

"Good for you all," Ms. Kennedy says. "You used several pieces of information found in sentences throughout the passage to help you figure out a word that was at first hard for you."

Rita explains, "Once I knew what *frail* meant, I could see how the purse was too heavy for him."

"Great," Ms. Kennedy replies. "So when you aren't sure what a word means, read many sentences around it to see if it gets clearer for you. Let's look at a few other words and use the context, or sentences around the word, to see if we can get clues to the meaning."

The students and Ms. Kennedy continue this type of investigation, searching the text for context to help them understand additional phrases and words like *blue-jean sitter* and *mistrusted* that were interfering with their deep comprehension. While *blue-jean sitter* was not a phrase that was needed to unlock the deepest understanding, Ms. Kennedy wanted these students to learn to use context to unlock the meaning of words and phrases. She also wanted them to pay close attention to the descriptive language the author used so they would develop a greater sensitivity to the power of selecting just the right words to express meaning. Once she felt secure that these three students had a deeper understanding of the text, she invited them to join the others to complete the larger group task.

Modeling Through Think-Alouds

As we've noted throughout this book, students are sometimes challenged by the meaning of the text because of the ambiguous nature of its language. Similarly, the tone may cause students confusion since they cannot understand the difference between irony and the literal meanings. One way teachers can model this for students is in a think-aloud. By thinking aloud about a text, especially the language that is used, students can hear an expert reader and thinker make meaning. The thinking aloud that teachers do during a small-group contingency lesson following a whole-group close reading lesson should be very focused and brief. The teacher should make obvious to the students what part of the text is being addressed and why he or she is modeling. Students can see how the teacher marks the text and how the marks relate to the language the teacher is using to make meaning of the text.

The following example illustrates using modeling through think-alouds while annotating the text to support small-group differentiated scaffolding. The rest of the class engages in an extension activity after a whole-class close reading. Eighth-grade health teacher Lee Enriquez selects a short article titled "How Much Technology Should You Let Your Children Use?" (Rosen, 2013) for the entire class to read. During the close reading, most of the students are able to identify how the author's use of language in the article gives the reader evidence of the bias he holds about technology. However, four students are not attending to the article's language and allow their own personal biases to interfere with the authors' point of view. Mrs. Enriquez asks the four students to join her at the back table so she can think aloud and annotate during reading to model how to specifically focus on the language of the text. Her purpose is to help them attend to the text's language so they can infer the author's message. But before beginning work with the smaller group, she asks the larger group of students to address the sentence, "Technology is a double-edged sword," by proposing an app or a commercial that could alert other students to the positive and negative effects of technology. As the larger group begins working, she meets with the group of four. Her meeting will be brief because she wants these students to also work on the extension task.

Two students gather on either side of her and observe how her written and spoken words work together to uncover the author's point of view.

Mrs. Enriquez begins: "Let's look closely at this section right here. I am interested to know what the author is saying and believing about technology and young children. I am going to put my personal feelings aside for the time being and see what language the author uses to clue me in to his opinions. Let's look. Right here it says it 'keeps them from spending time with their parents.' The author used the words 'keeps them from.' That tells me he doesn't like it. If he liked it he might use words like *they get to*—that would sound more positive. I'm going to underline that phrase and write the words *negative; against it* in the margin. Let me keep reading. 'You don't have a sense of the context, you don't have an understanding.' These are again negative phrases. He doesn't like technology for young children. The words 'don't' and 'not' are key words here. Just skimming the text I can see more phrases like 'not sufficient' and 'does not allow.' These are all phrases that paint a picture of someone who has a strong point of view and opinion—someone who doesn't believe that this kind of screen time is good for young children."

After the four students watch Mrs. Enriquez annotate as she thinks out loud, she invites them to read the next section and to underline the words and phrases that further indicate the author's position. She reminds them that this is exactly what she did when she was modeling for them. Mrs. Enriquez can tell that at first the students skim and scan, checking for positive or negative connotative words but then reread the short passage to get at the deeper message the author is conveying. As Mrs. Enriquez observes their annotations and later listens to the students' conversation, she is convinced that this quick ten-minute interaction with these students focused them more on the language the author uses. For example, when Brian highlights the phrase from the text, "behind a screen you do not see anyone but yourself reflected back" and writes "needs balance" in the margin, Ms. Enriquez determines that he is attending to the author's language to identify the author's message. Her assessment of the others' annotations indicates that they are also connecting the author's language and messages.

In their small group, the students received scaffolded instruction by hearing and seeing how an expert thinks about the text and how one's annotations support the insights he or she is developing about the text. Their subsequent performance made visible that they now understand how to attend to an author's language to infer the author's message and purpose. Mrs. Enriquez determines these students can now begin the extension task with the whole group.

Graphic Organizers

Students often use graphic organizers because teachers supply them in anticipation of potential challenges. There are many types of graphic organizers that support students making meaning of text. We understand that students often need to be given a graphic organizer to support their meaning making. However, we invite you to empower your students to create and design graphic organizers as needed for the types of text challenges they are facing.

For example, if students are stuck on a particular word, they should be encouraged to design a graphic organizer in the margin of their close reading text that would help them unlock the meaning of a word as they read. They can begin by setting up a chart and asking themselves what they know about the word. They may be able to define the word by identifying its part of speech from the context, its affix, or some of the words in the surrounding text. By knowing these three pieces of information about the word, a student could create a quick four-column chart (see table 7.2) on their paper's margin that could help them define the word and, by doing so, unlock the meaning of a challenging part of the text.

Table 7.2: Four-Column Graphic Organizer

Word	Part of Speech	Meaning of Affix (Prefix or Suffix)	Context Clues

For example, when a fourth grade class studying animal structure and biodiversity read an excerpt from *The Pier at the End of the World* (Erickson & Martinez, 2014), the readers could unlock the meaning of words like *contracts* and *inflated* by designing their graphic organizer in the margin and using the context to help them identify word meaning. The idea is to empower the reader to create this graphic organizer as needed to support his or her understanding of an unknown word that leads him or her to a deeper understanding. Soraya, a student in the class, uses such a graphic organizer to decipher those aforementioned terms in this section of a text: "Sometimes soft coral contracts into a lump. Then, when the ocean currents flow, it fills with seawater and blossoms into the shape of a miniature branching tree. Once inflated, it catches and eats plankton using its tiny tentacles" (p. 30).

Soraya puts the term *contracts* into her margin graphic organizer and then indicates that it is a verb. She knows from her study of affixes that *con* means *together*. Finally, looking at context clues, *coral contracts into a lump*, she visualizes a big mass of material coming together to form a ball, like a lump of coal. Through this analysis using a graphic organizer, Soraya goes beyond a definition she might find in a dictionary. She is able to generate a relevant image of an animal, coral, coming together in ball-like form. She uses this strategy to next help decipher the meaning of *inflated*. She knows that *inflate* is an action word—a verb—and she determines that the prefix *in* actually means *in*. At first, Soraya thinks that *inflate* might mean that the animal came inward, but then she looks over the context clues and notices that the text says, "when the ocean currents flow, it fills with seawater and blossoms into the shape of a miniature branching tree." She reconsiders her idea and determines that seawater was flowing into the animal to make it bigger, growing like branches of a tree. Soraya is empowered to independently extract word meaning using the mechanism of a well-crafted graphic organizer.

If your students have not had a lot of experience with graphic organizers, you may want to provide a few and explain how they are used. Then, using the complex text from the close reading, model how to complete them, guide students to fill one out with you, and check for understanding by having them complete a section on their own. The goal is to teach students about organization by using the graphic organizer as a tool to support text analysis. We need to develop agency with our students as they determine which graphic organizer is needed at which time.

Using graphic organizers as scaffolds during and after a close reading helps students unlock the meaning of tricky vocabulary words or difficult concepts. Graphic organizers can also be introduced as contingency scaffolds to support readers who have not initially comprehended a text during close reading. Figures 7.1–7.5 (pages 130–132) present some graphic organizers you may want to use to help students make sense of text when language is an obstacle. As we shared in chapter 2, students must have a grasp of language use and register if they are to move beyond a surface or general understanding of the text. When calling a smaller group of students together to share contingency scaffolds as a way to support their deep comprehension, teachers may choose to use these graphic organizers to help students unlock the meaning of some of the vocabulary or language that is getting in the way of their understanding. Often, students may know a bit about a word but can't give a complete definition for it. Having these insights is important for teachers in order to meet their students at their point of entry and build students' knowledge from what they already know.

Figure 7.1 (page 130) illustrates the Frayer model, which Dorothy A. Frayer, Wayne C. Fredrick, and Herbert J. Klausmeier (1969) developed to help students better understand vocabulary by including multiple dimensions of a word.

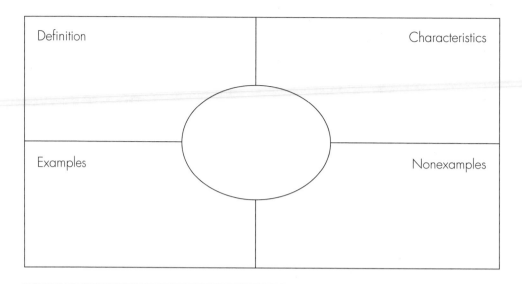

Figure 7.1: Frayer model.

Figure 7.2 is an alternate version of the Frayer model that many teachers use instead of the original model. Teachers sometimes use this version because they are more interested in having students study the characteristics of a topic rather than the definition of a word. This works well when students are exploring topics in science with different characteristics, such as animal types: mammals, reptiles, birds, insects, fish, and amphibians. Notice that in each of these graphic organizers the reader is supported in moving beyond a general definition of a term as they analyze its characteristics and also identify examples and nonexamples. A reader who knows which of these to use is one who understands the difference between understanding a word and a topic of study.

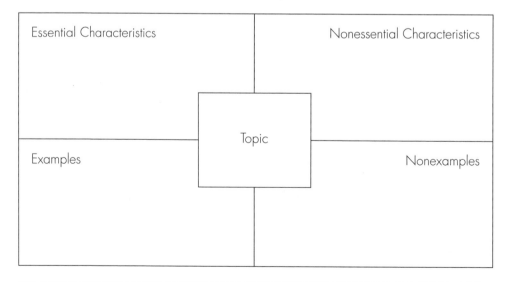

Figure 7.2: Alternate form of a Frayer graphic organizer to support understanding a topic rather than a word.

Figure 7.3 builds on these but invites the reader to also include his or her knowledge about the target word.

Unknown Word	What I Think I Know About the Word	What I Think the Word Looks Like	Words and Phrases From the Text to Support My Thinking

Figure 7.3: Graphic organizer for unknown words.

The following example illustrates using graphic organizers to support small-group differentiated scaffolding. Fifth-grade teacher Denise Freeman calls four students to work with her because the language of the text is getting in the way of their understanding during a close reading. To scaffold instruction for this group, she chooses to use a graphic organizer like the one featured in figure 7.3 because she has evidence from students' annotations that the words that are confusing them are not completely unfamiliar. This group still needs some explicit instruction with word structure. The students are reading a text on emergency planning and preparedness. Figure 7.4 is an example of one student's completed organizer, which helped him understand the word *reunification* that had originally caused him some confusion.

Unknown Word	What I Think I Know About the Word	What I Think the Word Looks Like	Words and Phrases From the Text to Support My Thinking
reunification	re = again unify = together		reunited not separated

Figure 7.4: Fifth-grade student work sample of graphic organizer for unknown words.

Ms. Freeman also created an additional graphic organizer (figure 7.5, page 132) to support students learning about complex text language.

Educators like Ms. Freeman have instructional targets of supporting all of their students in gaining the skills needed to read complex texts. When, during another close reading, Ms. Freeman sees a student from this small group creating her own graphic organizer (figure 7.6, page 133) to support her reading of an article about how mind exercise can improve mathematics scores (Oaklander, 2015), she feels secure that her students are gaining the skills they need to analyze complex texts.

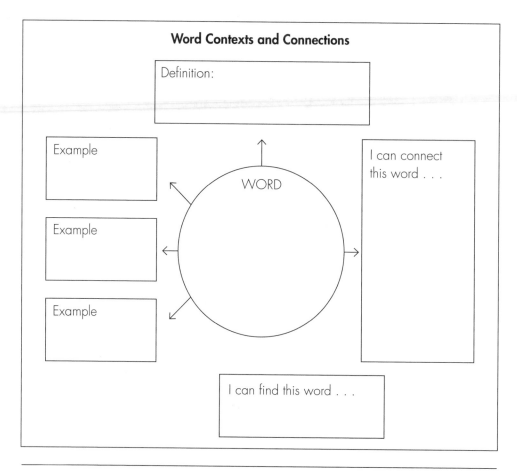

Figure 7.5: Word contexts and connections graphic organizer to support word analysis.

Visual Text

Some students benefit from illustrations provided within a text that allow them to "see" what words are on the page. Visual representation allows these students to understand the deepest meaning of the text more comprehensively. However, not every word, phrase, or language choice that appears in a text can be represented in the illustrations a book includes, and many texts may not include illustrations at all.

For these students, teachers may need to illustrate a text in additional ways. Using a visual text for a group of students as a differentiated scaffold following a whole-class reading might be exactly what students who struggle with the language need. A teacher could use images from the Internet, video clips, teacher sketches, or *realia* (real things or objects) to make some of the tricky words become more concrete and accessible. After the teacher shows the visual representation of a word, his or her students may even sketch their own representation on a whiteboard or paper to solidify the meaning of the word. The following scenario illustrates using visual text to support small-group differentiated scaffolding for understanding what the text means.

Fourth and fifth graders who did mindfulness exercises had 15% better math scores than their peers

In adults, mindfulness has been shown to have all kinds of amazing effects throughout the body; it can combat stress, protect your heart, shorten migraines and possibly even extend life. But a new trial published in the journal *Developmental Psychology* suggests that the effects are also powerful in kids as young as 9—so much so that improving mindfulness showed to improve everything from social skills to math scores. (Oaklander, 2015)

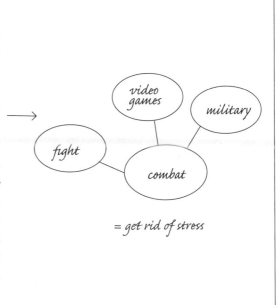

Figure 7.6: Graphic organizer created by a fifth grader.

High school art teacher Brad Phillips invites his class of twelfth graders to do a close reading of a blog post about Impressionist art (Impressionist Techniques, n.d.). Most of his students successfully read this complex text. The language, although challenging and domain specific, does not prevent most readers from understanding the text. However, some students do struggle with the language describing the Impressionist technique, as several question marks they make beside words and phrases on their copy of the text indicate.

At the conclusion of the reading, Mr. Phillips knows that he needs to invite a smaller group to work with him so he can scaffold the students' understanding. As he works with this smaller group, most of the class works in teams to practice the painting form and research artists who use this style in their works of art. With the smaller group, Mr. Phillips shares additional visual representations of Impressionist painters' techniques to help students connect the language on the page with the images. He encourages them to quickly sketch what they see in the visual representation next to the tricky words on their copy of the close reading text so they can connect the language of the text to the visual representation.

For example, the students in this small group all have difficulty with the word *juxtaposed*. It is interfering with their understanding of Impressionist painting techniques. Matthew makes marks on his paper, side by side in orange and blue, being careful not to mix the marks (or colors) on his paper. This sketch is placed right next to the sentence, "Colors are juxtaposed side-by-side with as few mixing as possible to create a vibrant color temperature where the colors mix in the eye of the beholder" (Impressionist Techniques, n.d.). By having the visual representation right next to the tricky word and sentence,

Matthew can refer to his sketch to help create meaning. Dori also tries this strategy but uses the colored pencils that are available at all work spaces in this art class. She uses the blue and red colored pencils to make marks on her paper, similar to Matthew's, where the colors sit side by side and do not mix.

After the students in this small group have tried this strategy of sketching visual representations during a close reading, it is clear to Mr. Phillips that they have a complete understanding of the complex text. Because he can see through the students' responses and annotations that they are able to answer his text-dependent question, What techniques are used by painters of Impressionism?, he is confident that they are ready to join the rest of the class as they practice Impressionist painting and research artists who use the technique.

Word Sorts

Word sorts engage students in analyzing words by sorting them into categories the teacher or the student identifies. Sorts provide students with multiple exposures to selected words and require them to think about the words from a particular perspective. Word sorts help students develop an analytical and in-depth knowledge of words, which is especially beneficial for striving readers. One way teachers can engage students in a focused lesson about language and its use is by having them write words they encountered in the close reading that were difficult and then work with the students to categorize words that have similar characteristics. Word sorts can be done on small individual whiteboards, with paper and a pencil, or on small slips of paper that students manipulate into particular categories.

Let's look at an example to see how Phyllis Pham uses word sorts with a group of second graders who struggled with the language in the whole-class close reading lesson using *The Recess Queen* (O'Neill, 2002). In a small group, Ms. Pham has the students write the character traits on slips of paper and group them into categories. Students are successful with some words. They know the following words are characteristic of Mean Jean: *bossy, mean, bully*. They also know that "bolted quick as lightning" and "bounced away" describe Katie Sue's behaviors. With a careful examination of the remaining slips of paper, students can see that "thundered close behind" is similar to the words they had previously assigned to Mean Jean. They also connect the phrase "gaped and stared" to Mean Jean since those "words are bad. When you stare it's bad, and we know that Mean Jean is bad, so we should put this slip of paper in this pile."

Students are able to make connections between words and phrases by categorizing and sorting their meanings into distinct groups. These kinesthetic and visual ways of meaning making help students internalize words and gain the information they need to understand the characters' traits.

Word Work

When closely reading a complex text, some students may misunderstand the meaning of words in the text because of their lack of knowledge about prefixes and suffixes. By asking questions that cause students to analyze these word parts, teachers may be able to eliminate this misunderstanding during the whole-class close reading lesson. A few students may also need to meet as a small group to explicitly support their understanding of how words work. Some students need explicit teaching to understand that prefixes are a word part with a specific meaning at the beginning of a word, while suffixes are a word part with a specific meaning at the end of a word. Teachers may need to teach students how to unlock the meaning of words by teaching them prefixes and suffixes. Teachers can do this by drawing students' attention to the prefix or suffix and isolating it from the root word. Students could very well be confused by the meanings of words because of the length of the word. Sometimes, by separating the word parts and attending to the structure of the word, students are less overwhelmed. Using a prefix/suffix dictionary is also a way students can learn the structures of words. When working with a teacher individually or in a small group, students can add prefixes like *epi*, *para*, and *trans* to a personalized dictionary that may include prefixes and suffixes that are challenging to them. Some teachers create charts with students so the students can see clearly how some prefixes and suffixes have similar meanings. (See figure 7.7.) These charts can hang in the classroom or be shrunk and kept in students' desks for when they need support.

Not	Between
il = illegal	inter = interact
im = impossible	intra = intranet
in = indefinite	

Figure 7.7: Prefix meaning chart.

Teachers may also want to use a Foldable to clearly show students how prefixes and suffixes can unlock and change the meaning of words. Take a look at the Foldable in figure 7.8, and notice how just by a flip of the flap the meaning of the word changes.

Figure 7.8: Foldable sample.

By focusing students' attention on these word parts, teachers can help students hone in on smaller units of meaning and see how, although small in size, these units can have a big impact on the meaning of the word.

The following example illustrates using word sorts to support small-group differentiated scaffolding. After the third graders in LeeAnn Lopez's classroom finish closely reading a text, Ms. Lopez notices that three students struggled to understand the meaning of the text because of several multisyllabic words containing prefixes. After carefully analyzing some of the patterns of the students' annotations, Ms. Lopez realizes that a brief lesson explicitly teaching the structure of words would help these students. She works with the students for no more than ten minutes on identifying prefixes in words, breaking the words apart to identify known words, and reconnecting word parts to see the word whole again. Ms. Lopez has students make Foldables using the words *overpowers*, *overcharged*, and *overworked*. These are words that students identified in the text as being confusing. Students construct the Foldables, discuss the meanings, sketch a quick picture next to the words, and brainstorm other words that include the prefix *over* (*overachiever*, *overarching*, *overlook*). After meeting with the students briefly, Ms. Lopez is confident that this minilesson on the structure of words will help the students the next time they encounter not only words with *over* as the prefix but other words with prefixes as well.

Conclusion

Students often read a text quickly and are able to share a very literal understanding. However, analyzing the language and the way it was used, including the language patterns, language choices, structured presentation of the language, and the rhythm and flow of the language causes readers to understand the text more deeply and the author's purpose for sharing. Analysis of these features of the text's language supports readers noting paradoxes about presented information or character behaviors and intentions. They begin to make inferences about authors' choices and presentation modes. Evaluation of the author's intention can then occur. Throughout the close reading, teachers should share questioning scaffolds that help students understand the meaning of a text through an analysis of its language. For students who need additional support after the close reading, the differentiated scaffolds this chapter has explained work well when implemented with smaller groups of students to further support their deepening understanding of the text.

Supporting Knowledge Demands With Differentiated Scaffolds

8

Savvy teachers recognize that nothing is more important to student comprehension of content than the knowledge they already have about a topic (Marzano, 2004). Numerous studies have confirmed this relationship between background knowledge and achievement (Dochy, Segers, & Buehl, 1999; Hailikari, Katajavuori, & Lindblom-Ylänne, 2008; Hailikari, Nevgi, & Lindblom-Ylänne, 2007; Nagy, Anderson, & Herman, 1987). This knowledge is the foundation for all future learning and provides the proverbial hooks on which students can hang new learning about a topic. Background knowledge contributes to every reading experience and improves comprehension, creates and builds motivation and interest, and enhances understanding of vocabulary.

Types of background knowledge that influence text comprehension include experiential knowledge, topical knowledge, cultural knowledge, and literary knowledge.

- **Experiential knowledge:** Experiential knowledge is a powerful form of background knowledge. One of the authors, for example, visited the Museum of Tolerance in Los Angeles, California. The museum provides many activities that allow the visitor to experience the horrors of the Holocaust. Visitors are each given a card with a brief biography of a child who lived during this time; at the end of the visit they learn whether or not their child survived. In addition, the museum contains a room designed to look like the concrete buildings in which the victims lived. Holocaust survivors give presentations about their lives during this time. Experiences like these help students bring greater understanding to numerous texts during their study of this time period. Obviously, schools are limited in the number of these experiences they can provide, but they can have a powerful effect on student learning.

- **Topical knowledge:** Topical knowledge creates a reservoir of information that students can draw on when reading a text. Topical knowledge is especially important with informational texts and often represents a type of knowledge that students lack, and this may limit students' comprehension. For example, students often lack background knowledge of historical events like the Vietnam War or World War II. These events are not within the range of their experience and represent time periods that seem far removed to them. Other subjects, such as science, require different forms of topical knowledge that may include knowledge of the scientific method, key scientific concepts, academic vocabulary, and so on.

- **Cultural knowledge:** Cultural knowledge refers to knowledge of a culture that can impact text comprehension. This can refer to knowledge of people, places, and events in Western culture as well as to specific knowledge of other cultures. While students do not usually need to be a member of a specific culture to understand a book set in that culture, they may more readily understand the nuances and deeper meanings of the text with that knowledge. The graphic novel *American Born Chinese* (Yang, 2008), for example, contains many subtle references to Chinese culture. Chinese American students might be able to contribute to class understanding by explaining the references' significance in Chinese culture.

- **Literary knowledge:** Literary knowledge demands can also create comprehension gaps in readers. Modern texts, for example, are full of references to other texts, and students will often miss deep text meanings without recognition of these references. Even picture books for younger students contain these references. *Hey, Al* (Yorinks, 1987), a Caldecott Medal winner, is the story of a janitor who becomes discontented with his life and escapes to a tropical paradise with his dog Eddie. They decide to return to New York when they begin to turn into birds, having recognized that paradise is less than perfect. Al is soaring in the sky on his return home when Eddie falls into New York Harbor. The illustration contains a clear mythological reference to the story of Daedalus and Icarus, in which Daedalus creates wax wings for himself and his son but warns Icarus not to fly too close to the sun or his wings will melt. Icarus disregards his father and plunges into the sea, just like Eddie. This visual reinforces the story's theme that contentment can be better than striving. Introducing students to this mythological story will help them appreciate the layered meaning of this book even more.

A number of issues surrounding the teaching of background knowledge have emerged with the Common Core State Standards. A key tenet of close reading is that readers need to focus on text content rather than external sources like the reader's previous knowledge, the author's biography, or other information sources. Part of the reason for this text emphasis is the view that too much instructional time has been devoted to building background knowledge about topics students may already know (Shanahan, 2014a). Shanahan argues that before-reading activities that include twenty minutes of discussion about visiting the zoo, for example, where each student relates an anecdote about his experiences, may not be the best use of instructional time.

In addition, because, as Shanahan (2014a) notes, more advantaged students often have more background knowledge than disadvantaged ones because of more experiences, wider reading, and so on, some Common Core advocates feel that not talking about prior knowledge will bridge the gap between poor and rich students when they read and make all students accountable for the same information. However, prior knowledge plays a role in comprehension regardless of whether there is a discussion (Shanahan, 2014a).

Because of these concerns, some teachers think that activating background knowledge is not "allowed" with close reading. This is really not the case; it is the *positioning* and *quality* of the background building in the lesson that differ.

So what should background building look like in a close reading? Following are a few guidelines.

- **Initially, make sure background building is limited and appropriate:** You might limit background building to telling students the topic they will be reading about, background about the overall text if they are reading an excerpt from a longer work, or other essential information. Background building should also be appropriate. For example, asking students if they have ever had a stain on their clothes that they could not get out as a precursor to reading Lady Macbeth's "out, damned spot" soliloquy really does little to prepare students for reading this text about the nature of guilt (Jago, 2012).

- **Be aware that background knowledge can be culture specific:** This type of background knowledge may be important and necessary to comprehension of certain texts, as in the example of *American Born Chinese* (Yang, 2008) discussed earlier.

- **Don't activate prior knowledge that may present student misconceptions, especially in science:** Discussing these misconceptions may simply reinforce them. As Shanahan (2014b) says, "Prior knowledge is a two-edged sword—it can increase learning and it can encourage readers to impose their own beliefs on a text."

- **Give students a chance to have a go at the text before providing or activating too much background knowledge:** During this first reading, students may be able to use the context of the text itself to get the information they need. Other times, you may want to position background activities before or during student reading.

But when, how, and what kind of extended background-building experiences should teachers provide for students when the text's knowledge demands are clearly beyond the background students possess? Sometimes teachers need to build background for students who have little of the experiential, topical, cultural, or literary knowledge required for a particular text. In other instances, the teacher's role is not to *give* students background knowledge about a topic but to engage them in intentional instructional experiences that *activate* knowledge they may have, or contribute to their reservoir of knowledge about a topic, making them better prepared to read about it.

This chapter focuses on the five types of differentiated scaffolds for addressing background knowledge: (1) text-dependent questions, (2) visual supports (realia, photographs, videos, charts, maps, diagrams, and more), (3) think-alouds, (4) virtual learning experiences, and (5) paired texts. Teachers may select one or more of these scaffolds depending on students' needs. They must carefully consider where to position these scaffolds in ways that will best support their students.

Text-Dependent Questions

Careful use of questioning during close reading can help bridge student gaps in background knowledge. Questions should be closely connected to the concepts in the text rather than trivial, tangentially related ideas. These questions are often positioned after the first reading, since students need the opportunity to share their understandings by discussing the text in pairs and in the large group. This response to the first reading can help the teacher determine if students need additional background building and what the nature of that background building should be. The experience of the first reading can actually build background for students.

The following list provides examples of questions that might be used to build student background knowledge at strategic points during a close reading.

- Based on the title, what do you think this will be about and why?
- What do you know about this author and his or her work?
- What do you already know about this topic?
- What did you learn from the first, second, or third reading that can help you understand this text?
- What other texts have you read about this topic?
- How is this text similar to or different from other texts you have read on this topic?
- How do the details in this text connect to what you already know?
- Have you ever read or seen something that reminds you of this text? What was it like?
- Have you ever had something like this happen to you? How did you feel?
- How can you create an analogy between what you've learned about and something you already know?
- Where could you go to learn more about this topic?
- What did you find out from your search, and how does it connect to the text?

The following scenario features Maria Gomez using questioning during a close reading in her classroom. Ms. Gomez is using the book *Starfish* (Hurd, 2000) for a first-grade close reading. She analyzes the text for complexity and identifies text language and the knowledge demands of the text as potential areas of need and creates the following text-dependent questions as scaffolds for learning.

- What is a starfish? (general understanding)
- What two words does the author use to tell us how starfish move on their feet? (vocabulary)
- Which body parts do starfish have and not have? (key details)
- Who is telling us the information, the starfish or a narrator? How do you know? (author's purpose)
- Why did the author write the book? To entertain or inform? (author's purpose)
- How do starfish find food and feed themselves? (inference) (Lapp et al., 2013, p. 114)

After her first read-aloud, she listens in on students' paired conversations in response to the question What is a starfish? and quickly recognizes that most students do not initially grasp the key concepts in this informational text. Many students incorrectly conclude that the text is about a trip to the seashore and completely miss the deep and complex information provided about starfish.

Most students have never seen a starfish, have never been to the ocean, and are unfamiliar with the habits of these sea creatures. Ms. Gomez proceeds to build background knowledge through text-based questioning for the *entire* group during each reading because most students lack the topical and linguistic background they need to succeed with this text. In other cases, she might save these strategies for use with a small group of students.

She decides to question students in ways that might activate and build on the background knowledge that they got from her first read-aloud. In thinking about what they might already know, she focuses on the word *starfish*. She says, "Let's take a look at the word *star*. What is a star? Where have you seen stars? What do they look like? Can anyone draw a star?" After one student draws a star on the document camera, she asks students to notice details about a star, including how many points it has and how it is constructed. She then asks students about the second part of the compound word, *fish*. She asks her students what they know about fish, where they find fish, and how fish live. Her students know that fish live in water and that they swim. Armed with this information, she asks them, "What do you think a fish that looks like a star might be like? Think about what you know about fish and what you learned from listening to the book I read to you earlier." Students suggest that a starfish might swim, it might live in water, it might have five points, and it might have legs. She records this information on a chart and uses this background as the basis for the next text reading, which focuses on helping students identify additional characteristics of starfish.

With older students who need background building or knowledge activation, questioning strategies like a carousel walk (Lent, 2012) can be helpful. Teachers can position this strategy before or after the first reading, depending on student needs. To prepare for a carousel walk, the teacher should carefully analyze the text at hand and identify important concepts or terms. She can then list key words or terms and record each one on a piece of chart paper. For example, if students have completed a first reading of an excerpt from *The Odyssey* and need more background knowledge, she might list questions like What is a Trojan horse?, What is a Cyclops?, and How would you describe the word *journey*? Students work in groups of three, and each group has a different marker. Each group then records what it knows about each term and then moves to the next paper and records ideas on it using its designated color marker. At this point, students return to their original papers and report on what each group wrote, asking for clarification or comments (Lent, 2012). Through this activity, students pool their knowledge and share it. They learn from one another, and the teacher learns what they know, what they don't know, and what misconceptions they may have.

Visual Supports

When students lack background knowledge, providing visual supports can be an effective, efficient means of building that knowledge. By analyzing visual texts, students sharpen their visual-literacy skills and can connect what they see to the text they will read. Visual supports can include realia, photographs, videos, charts, maps, diagrams, and more.

Realia give students the chance to use all their senses in learning (Echevarria, Vogt, & Short, 2010), and these sensory experiences can contribute to comprehension. Using realia lets students see, touch, and experience things from the physical world that can let them connect text content to real objects. Talking about these objects also develops oral language skills at the same time it builds topical knowledge. Furthermore, by talking about these objects, students learn vocabulary critical to understanding content.

Photographs also provide rich opportunity for background building. Primary-source photographs, for example, can provide historical perspectives that connect students to the past. Questioning students or thinking aloud about photographs of all types can deepen their understanding. With the vast array of visual resources available on the Internet, it is easier than ever for teachers to locate supportive visuals for students. Other excellent sources for photographs are children's, young adult, and informational trade books. An example of using visual supports to scaffold background knowledge, again using Ms. Gomez's lesson on *Starfish*, follows.

After she activates students' basic conceptual knowledge about starfish following the first text read-aloud, Ms. Gomez asks students to listen to the text a second time, focusing on the question, Which body parts do starfish have and not have? She listens in as students discuss this question and determines that many of them are unable to answer it. She decides that prior to the second reading she will share realia with her students to support their listening and thinking during the second reading. Ms. Gomez takes students to a science classroom that has a starfish specimen. As students approach the table in small groups, Ms. Gomez asks them to look carefully at the starfish and talk to a partner about what they see. She invites students to touch the starfish and note how it feels. Students note the body parts of the starfish that they recognize. After this, she asks the question again, Which body parts do starfish have and not have? The students then record their notes on a Foldable using either words or pictures. She notes that students are now able to accurately identify body parts starfish have as well as those they don't have. Through the visual support provided by the starfish specimen, the children were able to effectively deepen their understanding of text content and demonstrate that understanding on their Foldable.

Think-Alouds

Another great way to build background knowledge with students is through thinking aloud. As we've noted in other contingencies we've shared, with the think-aloud strategy, teachers model for students the kind of thinking they can do as they explore written texts. This can similarly be done with visuals by making thinking visible to students in ways that help them activate background knowledge and connect new information to the existing information that is already part of their schema.

Ms. Gomez decides to extend student understanding of the starfish's characteristics by doing a think-aloud using a captioned photo from the National Geographic (n.d.) website. After the second reading, she realizes that many students lack background for understanding the academic vocabulary of the text. To address this need, she projects this photo on the document camera and thinks aloud about the image as well as the caption: "Here we have a photograph of a starfish. As it says in the title, starfish are also called *sea stars*. A photograph of something is a picture taken of something that is real. When I look at this photograph, I notice that the starfish looks like a star. I notice that this starfish has five arms. I can count each of the arms, one, two, three, four, five. In the book *Starfish* it says [she points to text] that these arms are called *rays*. So this starfish has five rays. I also remember that starfish have no legs. I see that this starfish has little points on its back. These points look like they would be prickly. I remember that in the book [she points to the sentence] it says 'Some starfish are prickly.' I think that this must be one of those prickly starfish. I also notice that this starfish is bright red. I remember from the book that starfish come in different colors like pink, grey, and purple. Now I want to look at the writing underneath the picture. This is called a *caption*. The caption says, 'Sea stars are purely marine animals, even using sea water instead of blood to pump nutrients throughout their bodies.' As I read this sentence, I think the word *marine* is kind of hard. But I know that *marine* means something to do with the sea, so it must mean that sea stars are sea animals. The next part of the sentence says that the sea star uses sea water, not blood, to pump nutrients, which means food, through their bodies. I know that humans use blood to pump nutrients through the body, but sea stars are different. They use the water in the sea instead of blood to get their food."

From this think-aloud, students learn about the shape, colors, and characteristics of a starfish and that starfish use sea water, instead of blood, to pump nutrients through their system, as noted in the photo caption. A think-aloud of such a photo models for students ways that they can connect the knowledge obtained from the text read aloud to what they see in the photograph, building on their background knowledge so that they can revisit *Starfish* with more content understanding. It also ensures they are meeting the requirement of the Framework for K–12 Science Education, which states, "Students should be asked to use diagrams, maps, and other abstract models as tools that enable them to elaborate on their own ideas or findings and present them to others" (National Research Council Committee on a Conceptual Framework for New K–12 Science Education Standards, 2012, p. 58). Following this activity, the children formed pairs and retold the information the teacher had provided, using appropriate terminology like *sea star*, *ray*, and *marine*. As she listened in on these retellings, Ms. Gomez was confident that students understood the text.

Virtual Learning Experiences

While direct experiences are one of the best ways for teachers to engage students in learning, it is often difficult, if not impossible, for schools to provide students with these experiences. The next best thing to direct experiences is virtual ones. With the range and variety of online resources available, teachers can provide students with virtual experiences they may not have otherwise.

Video clips, simulations, and virtual tours can provide virtual experiences that take students anywhere in the world. They provide rich visual imagery for establishing students' conceptual understanding. When using virtual learning experiences, it is important for teachers to establish a purpose for student viewing so that students know what to look for. In addition, teachers may want to stop the video they're showing periodically to clarify or think aloud about the information provided. Following the use of a virtual learning experience with paired talk ensures that students can use the academic language provided to reflect on what they have learned.

The following scenario, continued from Ms. Gomez's starfish lesson, illustrates a virtual learning experience. During the think-aloud with *Starfish*, the students have some difficulty understanding how the starfish eats with such a tiny mouth. Ms. Gomez asks the text-dependent question for the final whole-class close reading, How do starfish find food and feed themselves? While the illustrations in the text support student understanding of the answer to this question, Ms. Gomez feels that a virtual video experience might build greater depth of knowledge for this concept. She locates a video on YouTube from the Vancouver Aquarium (2012) titled *Sunflower Star Has Weird Way of Eating*. This video takes students virtually to the bottom of the sea, where they can clearly see the sunflower starfish that is described in the text as it envelops a clam and pulls the shell open to eat the inside. The undulating tiny tube feet referred to in the book are clearly visible in the video, and students can easily see how the starfish moves to capture its prey.

Before showing students the video, Ms. Gomez tells them that the purpose for viewing the video is to learn how a starfish can eat a clam with its tiny mouth. During the first viewing, she simply asks students to watch the video and share what they learn with a partner. She shows the video again, and follows up with several questions designed to draw connections between the video and the text. She asks, "What kind of starfish is this, and how do you know? Be sure to put a sticky note on the page where you found the answer." Students easily identify the sunflower starfish because of its many rays and its distinctive color. Ms. Gomez then asks students, "How did the starfish in the video move, and how do you know?" Again, students easily identify the tube feet that starfish use to move and cite evidence from both the text and the video to support their answers. She then asks students to view the video one more time and describe to a partner in their own words how the starfish eats the clam. Ms. Gomez then rereads the description in the text and asks students what they might add to that description based on what they saw in the video.

Following their virtual learning experience, students have deepened their background knowledge about the starfish's habits and behaviors. By virtually experiencing the starfish's activities at the bottom of the ocean, students contextualized their learning in ways that would not otherwise be possible. They were now well prepared to complete their final reading of the text and explore the question about how starfish find and eat their food.

After using questions, visual supports, think-alouds, and virtual learning experiences to support her students' emerging background knowledge, Ms. Gomez feels confident her students can continue the close reading lesson successfully. They are now able to answer increasingly complex questions and complete a follow-up writing assignment in which they write a minireport on what they have learned about starfish. Through her strategic use of scaffolds, Ms. Gomez creates a successful close reading lesson for these young readers.

Paired Texts

In addition to text-dependent questions, visual supports, think-alouds, and virtual learning experiences, teachers will sometimes need to turn to supportive companion texts to scaffold student learning from close reading texts. These companion texts can facilitate increased comprehension by supporting students who struggle with text language demands that are dependent upon background knowledge.

As we noted in chapter 5 (page 85), at times, some students' language and content connections may require scaffolding that involves a more accessible text before they can tackle a complex text. Another great reason for using paired texts is that the CCSS require students to synthesize ideas from multiple texts (NGA & CCSSO, 2010). Paired texts give students lots of experience in reading and studying an array of theme-related texts and media, which can help them make connections, determine themes across texts, and use newly learned content to write about compiled ideas. In the example that follows, we see how kindergarten teacher Carolyn Wenger decides to use a paired text as an instructional scaffold for a small group of kindergarten students who lack background knowledge on a concept central to understanding a text.

Mrs. Wenger's class is reading *How a Seed Grows* (Jordan, 1992). Prior to the lesson, she analyzes the text for complexity and finds that most aspects of text complexity could be rated as easy or at grade level. The key ideas and details in the text are fairly easy to grasp, vocabulary is well supported with context clues and illustrations, and the text structure is predominantly sequential. She pinpoints two areas that might be challenging: comprehending abstract ideas and inferring relationships among ideas. Her lesson purpose focuses on helping students identify and analyze the steps in the growth of a seed, a concept that is part of the science curriculum at her grade level. Mrs. Wenger carefully scaffolds her lesson to meet the needs of her many English learners who are completing a close reading and listening lesson for the first time. In addition, she makes contingency plans for using alternate texts in case her students need additional supports.

She begins her lesson by sharing the book on the document camera and having students listen to her read the first three pages of the text and share questions they have about the content with their partners. She records these on a list in front of the room. She then reads the next two pages, asking students, "Do all seeds grow at the same speed? How do you know?" She models for students how to find evidence for the answer and marks the text with a sticky note. She continues reading a few pages of text and then stopping, asking students to identify questions they have and locate evidence for additional text-dependent questions. The children put sticky notes on the text (annotate) to mark those answers.

For the second text reading, Mrs. Wenger chooses to reread five pages that focus on the steps in the bean-to-plant process. She asks students to listen carefully to identify the four steps in this process. She calls different students to the document camera to place sticky notes on the places in the text that describe each step. Following this, she gives students pictures of each step in the process. Students glue these on their papers in the proper order and use sequence words (*first, second, third, last*) they studied earlier to describe the process to a partner. She circulates around the room, checking for understanding by listening to students' descriptions of the process, and records anecdotal notes about each student's retelling. At this point, Mrs. Wenger does a careful analysis of student understanding of the bean-to-plant process. Her anecdotal notes reveal retellings ranging from "First it is a seed. Roots come out. The roots get bigger and bigger until the seed is pushed up and root hairs push down. Finally it has leaves and you know it is a plant" to responses like "seed, roots, stem, plant." She knows that students need deep understanding of this concept and need to be able to express their understanding through more detailed and elaborate retellings if they are to demonstrate true understanding of this process. This ability is foundational for the writing assignment Mrs. Wenger has planned for the culmination of the lesson.

For the larger group of students who are able to complete the retelling task, Mrs. Wenger pairs students and has them create a graphic organizer on which they draw pictures of the steps in the bean-to-plant process and record each step in writing. The graphic organizers are differentiated to address the different levels in the class. Some students complete sentence frames that say *first* _____, *next* _____, and so on, while other frames require that students simply fill in a single word or two in each sentence.

Mrs. Wenger realizes that a few of her students need further support in retelling the steps in the bean-to-plant process. She moves these students into a small group and introduces a creative dramatics lesson. The creative dramatics activity, while not a text in the traditional sense, serves as a paired text for the book because it provides a scaffold for student learning in a kinesthetic mode appropriate to the developmental level of kindergartners. Mrs. Wenger knows that creative dramatics can help these students picture the growth of the seed, develop oral language skills by using the academic language needed to understand the process, and become kinesthetically engaged in ways that can help them remember the content. She has students look again at their sequenced pictures of the steps and models for students how to act out each one. The students themselves begin to act out these steps under her direction. Then Mrs. Wenger helps the students describe to a partner what they dramatized during each step, using key sequencing words like *first, next, then,* and *finally.* She listens in on these conversations and notes that students are using more elaborate language in their retellings. In this way she supports students as they master academic vocabulary, deepen their conceptual knowledge, and increase their oral language skills by moving from simplistic retellings to elaborate, detailed ones.

After this differentiated scaffold, these students are prepared to join the larger group as they complete the close reading. For the final reading, she asks them to consider progressively more challenging questions: Why do some seeds grow better than others? Can you provide evidence for your answer? How is the life cycle of a plant similar to your growing up? By this time, students can address the knowledge demands of the text successfully and locate evidence and complete annotations with sticky notes in their own text copies.

Note how and when Mrs. Wenger chooses to use a paired text (creative dramatics) to provide differentiated scaffolds for students who need additional help. After using oral retelling as her formative assessment, she has clear evidence that some students need support and could not successfully continue the close reading without foundational knowledge about the bean-to-plant process. The creative dramatics activity she uses bridges student understanding gained from the first reading and prepares them for the subsequent readings and the final writing assessment.

The decision about how and when to use paired texts as an instructional contingency is one that good teachers make based on the challenges posed by the text and students' needs. There is no one way to use paired texts; it is up to you to make an informed decision about the instructional conditions under which this should happen as well as the optimal point for this intervention.

Conclusion

Multiple forms of background knowledge influence text comprehension, including experiential knowledge, topical knowledge, cultural knowledge, and literary knowledge. Many students lack these forms of background knowledge, and these gaps can interfere with comprehension, especially when students are engaging with the complex texts required for close reading. Scaffolded supports, including text-dependent questions, visual supports, think-alouds, virtual learning experiences, and paired texts can make even the most complex texts accessible to readers of all ages.

Epilogue

Differentiated scaffolds support every student's attempts to successfully read complex texts. Questions the teacher asks during the whole-group close reading are the initial scaffolds offered to the whole class. When these are not sufficient support for some students, contingent scaffolds need to be offered. These differentiated scaffolds often occur as the teacher works with this smaller group of students. The small-group format used in the majority of the scenarios throughout this text is often the perfect configuration for working with students who have not had initial success. The differentiated scaffolds offered within these small groups ensure that every student will acquire the skills, language, and information needed to analyze the text.

As we all grapple with the intricacies of planning and supporting close reading experiences, we cannot help but be aware of the differences in students in terms of their understanding of a text. This is not a new phenomenon. Learning differences are always obvious when students read texts. Differences occur for many reasons, including one's knowledge of vocabulary, the ways the author uses the nuances of language, the text structures and use of rhetorical devices, and the topic and student's interest in pursuing it as well as his or her proficiency as a reader. We continue to grow in our understanding of best practices that support students' close reading endeavors, and we hope the tools and insights we have offered will support your practice. Like yours, our goal is to promote reading success and the love of reading for every student.

Appendix A
Instructional Scenario Chart

We have included small-group scaffolded instructional scenarios throughout the text as examples of what can occur after a whole-group close reading experience when a few students have not comprehended the text. Please use the instructional scenario chart in table A.1 to find examples of contingency instruction designed to promote close reading success for every student. Column one identifies the grade level at which the small-group contingency instruction occurred. Columns two and three identify the chapter and page number to make finding these scenarios very time efficient, and column four identifies the focus of each instructional example.

Table A.1: Instructional Scenario Chart

Grade Level	Location	Page	Focus of Instructional Scenario Example
3	Chapter 2	17	Text complexity
6	Chapter 3	56	Text-dependent questions
8	Chapter 4	74	Close reading, assessment, contingency support planning
4	Chapter 5	90	Graphic organizer as a contingency support for what a text means
11	Chapter 5	92	Graphic organizer as a contingency support for what a text means
3	Chapter 5	94	Graphic organizer as a contingency support for what a text means
5	Chapter 5	101	Think-alouds as a contingency support for what a text means
7	Chapter 5	103	Paired texts as a contingency support for what a text means

CONTINUED →

Grade Level	Location	Page	Focus of Instructional Scenario Example
3	Chapter 6	108	Signal words as a contingency support for how a text works
3	Chapter 6	111	Multimedia as a contingency support for how a text works
10	Chapter 6	113	Vocabulary as a contingency support for how a text works
5	Chapter 6	116	Think-alouds as a contingency support for how a text works
6	Chapter 6	119	Text-dependent questions as a contingency support for how a text works
8	Chapter 7	127	Think-alouds as a contingency support for what a text means
4	Chapter 7	128	Graphic organizer as a contingency support for what a text means
12	Chapter 7	133	Visual texts as a contingency support for what a text means
2	Chapter 7	134	Word sorts as a contingency support for what a text means
1	Chapter 8	140	Text-dependent questions as a contingency support for knowledge demands
1	Chapter 8	142	Visual supports as a contingency support for knowledge demands
1	Chapter 8	143	Think-alouds as a contingency support for knowledge demands
1	Chapter 8	144	Virtual learning experiences as contingency support for knowledge demands
K	Chapter 8	145	Paired texts as a contingency support for knowledge demands
2	**go.SolutionTree .com/literacy**	n/a	Various word-work activities to support language learning
5	**go.SolutionTree .com/literacy**	n/a	Visual supports, paired text, rereading original text to support language learning, developing knowledge of topic text structure
10	**go.SolutionTree .com/literacy**	n/a	Graphic (paired) text to support understanding of textual language and organization

References and Resources

ACT. (2006). *Reading between the lines: What the ACT reveals about college readiness in reading.* Iowa City, IA: Author. Accessed at www.act.org/research/policymakers/pdf /reading_report.pdf on September 14, 2015.

Adams, M. J. (2010–2011). Advancing our students' language and literacy: The challenge of complex texts. *American Educator, 34*(4), 3–11, 53.

Adler, D. A. (2003). *Mama played baseball.* San Diego, CA: Gulliver Books.

Adler, M. J., & Van Doren, C. (1972). *How to read a book: The classic guide to intelligent reading* (Rev. and updated ed.). New York: Touchstone.

Allal, L. (1988). Vers un élargissement de la pédagogie de maîtrise: Processus de régulation interactive, rétroactive et proactive [Toward expanding the mastery learning: Interactive control process, retroactive and proactive]. In M. Huberman (Ed.), *Assurer la réussite des apprentissages scolaires? Les propositions de la pédagogie de maîtrise* [Ensure the success of academic learning? The proposals of the mastery learning] (pp. 86–126). Neuchâtel, Switzerland: Delachaux & Niestlé.

Allen, G. (2000). *Intertextuality.* London: Routledge.

Alternative Fuels Data Center. (n.d.). *Benefits and considerations of electricity as a vehicle fuel.* Accessed at www.afdc.energy.gov/fuels/electricity_benefits.html on September 14, 2015.

American Museum of Natural History. (2014). *Ocean: The definitive visual guide* (Rev. ed.). New York: Dorling Kindersley.

Anthony, S. B. (1873). *Woman's rights to the suffrage.* Accessed at www.nationalcenter .org/AnthonySuffrage.html on September 14, 2015.

Aquarium of the Pacific. (n.d.a). *Ammonite.* Accessed at www.aquariumofpacific.org /onlinelearningcenter/species/ammonite on September 14, 2015.

Aquarium of the Pacific. (n.d.b). *Chambered nautilus.* Accessed at www.aquariumof pacific.org/onlinelearningcenter/species/chambered_nautilus on September 14, 2015.

Arnold, T. (2005). *Hi! Fly guy.* New York: Cartwheel Books.

Atwater, R., & Atwater, F. (1988). *Mr. Popper's penguins.* Boston: Little, Brown.

Barden, C., & Backus, M. (2011). *Westward expansion and migration, grades 6–12.* Quincy, IL: Mark Twain Media.

Beers, K., & Probst, R. E. (2013). *Notice and note: Strategies for close reading.* Portsmouth, NH: Heinemann.

Berger, M. (1992). *Discovering Mars: The amazing story of the red planet.* New York: Scholastic.

Bintz, W. (2015). *Using paired texts to meet the Common Core: Effective teaching across the K–8 curriculum.* New York: Guilford Press.

Birch Aquarium at Scripps Institution of Oceanography. (n.d.). *Kelp cam—live!* [Video feed]. Accessed at http://aquarium.ucsd.edu/Education/Learning_Resources/Kelp _Cam on September 14, 2015.

Blundell, J. (2011). *Strings attached.* New York: Scholastic.

Boyne, J. (2007). *The boy in the striped pajamas.* New York: David Fickling Books.

Bransford, J. D., Brown, A. L., & Cocking, R. R. (Eds.). (2000). *How people learn: Brain, mind, experience, and school* (Expanded ed.). Washington, DC: National Academy Press.

Bressler, C. E. (2006). *Literary criticism: An introduction to theory and practice* (4th ed.). Upper Saddle River, NJ: Prentice Hall.

Brimner, L. D. (2014). *Strike!: The farm workers' fight for their rights.* Honesdale, PA: Calkins Creek.

Brown, D. (1970). *Bury my heart at Wounded Knee: An Indian history of the American West.* New York: Holt, Rinehart, & Winston.

Brown, S., & Kappes, L. (2012, October). *Implementing the Common Core State Standards: A primer on "close reading of text."* Washington, DC: Aspen Institute.

Brown v. Board of Education, 347 U.S. 483 (1954).

Brummett, B. (2010). *Techniques of close reading.* Thousand Oaks, CA: SAGE.

Bruner, J. S. (1966). *Toward a theory of instruction.* Cambridge, MA: Belknap Press.

Brush, T. A., & Saye, J. W. (2002). A summary of research exploring hard and soft scaffolding for teachers and students using a multimedia supported learning environment. *Journal of Interactive Online Learning, 1*(2), 1–12.

Bulla, C. R. (2001). *A tree is a plant.* New York: HarperCollins.

Carson, R. (1962). *Silent spring.* New York: Houghton Mifflin.

Chaucer, G. (1992). *Canterbury tales.* New York: Everyman's Library. (Original work published 1472)

Cherokee Nation. (n.d.). Letter from Chief John Ross. In G. E. Moulton (Ed.), *The papers of chief John Ross* (vol. 1, 1807–1839). Norman: University of Oklahoma Press. Accessed at www.cherokee.org/AboutTheNation/History/TrailofTears/ LetterfromChiefJohnRoss.aspx on September 14, 2015.

The Civil Rights Act of 1964, Public Law 88–352, 88th Cong., 2nd sess., H.R. 7152, July 2, 1964, § 201(a).

Clark, K. F., & Graves, M. F. (2005). Scaffolding students' comprehension of text. *Reading Teacher, 58*(6), 570–580.

Clay, M. M. (2005). *Literacy lessons designed for individuals: Designed for individuals— Part two, teaching procedures.* Portsmouth, NH: Heinemann.

Cline-Ransome, L. (2012). *Words set me free: The story of young Frederick Douglass.* New York: Simon & Schuster Books for Young Readers.

Cornell Sugar Maple Research and Extension Program. (n.d.a). *Making a new tree: Reproduction and cloning.* Accessed at http://maple.dnr.cornell.edu/kids /reproduction.htm on June 2, 2015.

Cornell Sugar Maple Research and Extension Program. (n.d.b). *Red maple.* Accessed at http://maple.dnr.cornell.edu/kids/tree_red.htm on June 5, 2015.

Cornell Sugar Maple Research and Extension Program. (n.d.c). *Sugar maple.* Accessed at http://maple.dnr.cornell.edu/kids/tree_sug.htm on June 5, 2015.

Cross, K. P. (1999, June). *Learning is about making connections* (Cross Paper No. 3). Mission Viejo, CA: League for Innovation in the Community College.

Curtis, C. P. (1999). *Bud, not Buddy.* New York: Delacorte Press.

DiCamillo, K. (2013). *Flora and Ulysses: The illuminated adventures.* Somerville, MA: Candlewick Press.

Dickinson, D. K., & Tabors, P. O. (2001). *Beginning literacy with language: Young children learning at home and school.* Baltimore, MD: P. H. Brookes.

Dochy, F., Segers, M., & Buehl, M. M. (1999). The relationship between assessment practices and outcomes of studies: The case of research on prior knowledge. *Review of Educational Research, 69*(2), 147–186.

Douglass, F. (2001). *Narrative of the life of Frederick Douglass, an American slave, written by himself* (J. W. Blassingame, J. R. McKivigan, & P. P. Hinks, Eds.). New Haven, CT: Yale University Press. (Original work published 1845)

Echevarria, J., Vogt, M., & Short, D. J. (2010). *Making content comprehensible for elementary English learners: The SIOP model.* Boston: Allyn & Bacon.

Ellis, D. (2001). *The breadwinner.* Berkeley, CA: Publishers Group West.

Engelbert, P. (2009). *Astronomy and space: From the big bang to the big crunch.* Farmington Hills, MI: Gale Cengage Learning.

Erickson, P., & Martinez, A. (2014). *The pier at the end of the world.* Thomaston, ME: Tilbury House Publishers.

Fisher, D., & Frey, N. (2014a). *Checking for understanding* (2nd ed.). Alexandria, VA: ASCD.

Fisher, D., & Frey, N. (2014b). Contingency teaching during close reading. *The Reading Teacher, 68*(4), 277–286.

Fisher, D., Frey, N. & Lapp, D. (2016). *Text complexity: Stretching readers with texts and tasks* (2nd ed.). Thousand Oaks, CA: Corwin.

Fraunhofer-Gesellschaft. (2015, June 11). Mini laser for real-time quality control. *ScienceDaily.* Accessed at www.sciencedaily.com/releases/2015/06/150611090351 .htm on September 14, 2015.

Frayer, D. A., Fredrick, W. C., & Klausmeier, H. J. (1969, April). *A schema for testing the level of concept mastery* (Working Paper No. 16). Madison: Wisconsin Research and Development Center for Cognitive Learning.

Gibbons, G. (1988). *Sunken treasure.* New York: HarperCollins.

Gibbons, G. (1994). *Nature's green umbrella: Tropical rain forests.* New York: Morrow Junior Books.

Giovanni, N. (1996). Covers. In *The sun is so quiet* (pp. 8–9). New York: Holt.

Giovanni, N. (2007). A poem for my librarian, Mrs. Long. In *Acolytes* (p. 91). New York: William Morrow.

Goldman, S. R., & Lee, C. D. (2014). Text complexity: State of the art and the conundrums it raises. *Elementary School Journal, 115*(2), 290–300.

Gray, T. (2014). *Molecules: The elements and the architecture of everything.* New York: Black Dog and Leventhal.

Grimm, J., & Grimm, W. (1944). *The complete Grimm's fairy tales*. New York: Pantheon.

Guthrie, J. T., & Cox, K. E. (2001). Classroom conditions for motivation and engagement in reading. *Educational Psychology Review, 13*(3), 283–302.

Hailikari, T., Katajavuori, N., & Lindblom-Ylänne, S. (2008). The relevance of prior knowledge in learning and instructional design. *American Journal of Pharmaceutical Education, 72*(5), 113. Accessed at http://dx.doi.org/10.5688/aj7205113 on March 21, 2016.

Hailikari, T., Nevgi A., & Lindblom-Ylänne, S. (2007). Exploring alternative ways of assessing prior knowledge, its components and their relation to student achievement: A mathematics-based case study. *Studies in Educational Evaluation, 33*, 320–337.

Hawking, S. (1988). *A brief history of time: From the big bang to black holes*. New York: Bantam Books.

Henkes, K. (1996). *Lilly's purple plastic purse*. New York: Greenwillow Books.

Hersey, J. (1989). *Hiroshima*. New York: Vintage.

Hiebert, E. H., & Pearson, P. D. (2014). Understanding text complexity: Introduction to the special issue. *Elementary School Journal, 115*(2), 153–160.

Hinchman, K. A., & Moore, D. W. (2013). Close reading: A cautionary interpretation. *Journal of Adolescent and Adult Literacy, 56*(6), 441–450.

Hinds, G. (2015). *Macbeth: A graphic novel adapted and illustrated by Gareth Hinds based on the play by William Shakespeare*. Somerville, MA: Candlewick Press.

Hirsch, E. D., Jr. (2006). *The knowledge deficit: Closing the shocking education gap for American children*. New York: Houghton Mifflin.

Hoffman, M., & Binch, C. (2000). *Boundless Grace*. New York: Puffin Books.

Holston, V., & Santa, C. (1985). RAFT: A method of writing across the curriculum that works. *Journal of Reading, 28*(5), 456–457.

Hurd, E. T. (2000). *Starfish*. New York: HarperCollins.

Impressionist Techniques. (n.d.). *The technique*. Accessed at https://impressioniststech.wordpress.com/the-technique on September 14, 2015.

International Reading Association. (n.d.). *Literacy implementation guidance for the ELA Common Core State Standards*. Accessed at www.literacyworldwide.org/docs/default-source/where-we-stand/ela-common-core-state-standards-guidance.pdf?sfvrsn=8 on February 25, 2015.

Isaacson, P. M. (1993). *A short walk through the pyramids and through the world of art.* New York: Alfred A. Knopf.

Jacobs, A., & Jacobs, K. (n.d.). *A virtual tour of Auschwitz/Birkenau.* Accessed at http://remember.org/auschwitz/index.html on May 20, 2015.

Jago, C. (2012, November). Closer reading for deeper comprehension: Uncommon sense about the Common Core. *AdLit in Perspective.* Accessed at www.ohiorc.org/adlit/inperspective/issue/2012-10/Article/feature.aspx on June 4, 2015.

Jenkins, S. (2014). *Eye to eye: How animals see in the world.* Boston: Houghton Mifflin Harcourt Publishing.

Jordan, H. J. (1992). *How a seed grows.* New York: HarperCollins.

Kalman, B., & Smithyman, K. (2002). *The life cycle of a tree.* New York: Crabtree.

Kintsch, W. (1998). *Comprehension: A paradigm for cognition.* New York: Cambridge University Press.

Koscielniak, B. (2004). *About time: A first look at time and clocks.* New York: Houghton Mifflin.

Kudlinski, K. V. (2005). *Boy, were we wrong about dinosaurs!* New York: Dutton Children's Books.

Kurland, D. (n.d.). *Three ways to read and discuss texts.* Accessed at www.criticalreading.com/ways_to_read.htm on December 14, 2014.

Lapp, D. (2012). *IRA E-ssentials: Teaching students to closely read texts: How and when?* Newark, DE: International Reading Association. Accessed at www.reading.org/general/Publications/e-ssentials/e8022 on September 14, 2015.

Lapp, D., Fisher, D., Frey, N., & Gonzalez, A. (2014). Students can purposefully create information, not just consume it. *Journal of Adolescent and Adult Literacy, 58*(3), 182–188.

Lapp, D., Grant, M., Moss, B., & Johnson, K. (2013). Students' close reading of science texts: What's now? What's next? *Reading Teacher, 67*(2), 109–119.

Lapp, D., Moss, B., Grant, M., & Johnson, K. (2015). *A close look at close reading: Teaching students to analyze complex texts, grades K–5.* Alexandria, VA: Association for Supervision and Curriculum Development.

Lapp, D., Wolsey, T. D., & Wood, K. (2015). *Mining complex text, grades 2–5: Using and creating graphic organizers to grasp content and share new understandings.* Thousand Oaks, CA: Corwin Press.

Lapp, D., Wolsey, T. D., Wood, K., & Johnson, K. (2015). *Mining complex text, grades 6–12: Using and creating graphic organizers to grasp content and share new understandings.* Thousand Oaks, CA: Corwin Press.

Lauber, P. (1996). *Hurricanes: Earth's mightiest storms.* New York: Scholastic.

Lent, R. C. (2012). Background knowledge: The glue that makes learning stick. In *Overcoming textbook fatigue: 21st century tools to revitalize teaching and learning* (pp. 30–49). Accessed at www.ascd.org/publications/books/113005/chapters/Background -Knowledge@-The-Glue-That-Makes-Learning-Stick.aspx on June 8, 2015.

Lester, H. (1988). *Tacky the penguin.* Boston: Houghton Mifflin.

Lewis, C. S. (2005). *The lion, the witch, and the wardrobe.* New York: HarperCollins. (Original work published 1950)

Lisa. (2011, February 28). *Featured poem: In a library by Emily Dickinson.* Accessed at http://thereaderonline.co.uk/2011/02/28/featured-poem-in-a-library-by-emily -dickinson on September 14, 2015.

Little, J. (1989). About feeling Jewish. In *Hey world, here I am!* (pp. 52–53). New York: Harper & Row.

Locker, M. (2014, December 16). This is how music can change your brain. *Time.* Accessed at http://time.com/3634995/study-kids-engaged-music-class-for -benefits-northwestern on September 15, 2015.

Maruki, T. (1980). *Hiroshima no pika.* New York: Lothrop, Lee & Shepard.

Marzano, R. J. (2004). *Building background knowledge for academic achievement: Research on what works in schools.* Alexandria, VA: Association for Supervision and Curriculum Development.

Metzger, E. P. (n.d.). *A model of sea-floor spreading teacher's guide.* Accessed at www .ucmp.berkeley.edu/fosrec/Metzger3.html on September 14, 2015.

Morgan, E. (2014). *Next time you see a maple seed.* Arlington, VA: National Science Teachers Association.

Moser, L. (2013). *Frequently asked questions.* Accessed at http://lisamoserbooks.com /faq.html on September 14, 2015.

Moss, B. (2012). Making the Common Core text exemplars accessible to middle graders. *Voices From the Middle, 20*(1), 62–65.

Moss, B., Lapp, D., Grant, M., & Johnson, K. (2015). *A close look at close reading: Teaching students to analyze complex texts, grades 6–12.* Alexandria, VA: Association for Supervision and Curriculum Development.

Murphy, J. (2010). *The great fire*. New York: Scholastic.

Nagy, W. E., Anderson, R. C., & Herman, P. A. (1987). Learning word meanings from context during normal reading. *American Educational Research Journal, 24*(2), 237–270.

National Council for the Social Studies (NCSS). (2013). *The college, career, and civic life (C3) framework for social studies state standards: Guidance for enhancing the rigor of K–12 civics, economics, geography, and history.* Silver Spring, MD: Author.

National Geographic. (n.d.). *Starfish (sea star).* Accessed at http://animals.national geographic.com/animals/invertebrates/starfish on June 10, 2015.

National Geographic Kids. (n.d.). *Geology 101.* Accessed at http://kids.national geographic.com/explore/science/geology-101 on September 14, 2015.

National Governors Association Center for Best Practices & Council of Chief State School Officers. (n.d.a). *Common Core State Standards for English language arts & literacy in history/social studies, science, and technical subjects: Appendix A—Research supporting key elements of the standards.* Washington, DC: Author. Accessed at www.corestandards.org/assets/Appendix_A.pdf on September 14, 2015.

National Governors Association Center for Best Practices & Council of Chief State School Officers. (n.d.b). *Common Core State Standards for English language arts & literacy in history/social studies, science, and technical subjects: Appendix B—Text exemplars and sample performance tasks.* Washington, DC: Author. Accessed at www.corestandards.org/assets/Appendix_B.pdf on September 14, 2015.

National Governors Association Center for Best Practices & Council of Chief State School Officers. (2010). *Common Core State Standards for English language arts and literacy in history/social studies, science, and technical subjects.* Washington, DC: Authors. Accessed at www.corestandards.org/assets/CCSSI_ELA%20Standards.pdf on September 14, 2015.

National Museum of American History. (n.d.). *The court's decision.* Accessed at http://americanhistory.si.edu/brown/history/5-decision/courts-decision.html on September 14, 2015.

National Research Council Committee on a Conceptual Framework for New K–12 Science Education Standards. (2012). *A framework for K–12 science education: Practices, crosscutting concepts, and core ideas.* Washington, DC: National Academies Press.

Newkirk, T. (2012). *The art of slow reading: Six time-honored practices for engagement.* Portsmouth, NH: Heinemann.

Next Generation Science Standards Lead States. (2013). *Next Generation Science Standards: For states, by states.* Washington, DC: National Academies Press.

Nicastro, M. (2008). *Circumference: Eratosthenes and the ancient quest to measure the globe*. New York: St. Martin's Press.

Niffenegger, A. (2003). *The time traveler's wife*. New York: Harcourt.

NOVA. (n.d.). *The Grand Canyon: Evidence of Earth's past* [Video file]. Accessed at www.pbslearningmedia.org/resource/ess05.sci.ess.earthsys.nautiloid/the-grand-canyon-evidence-of-earths-past on September 14, 2015.

Oaklander, M. (2015, January 26). Mindfulness exercises improve kids' math scores. *Time*. Accessed at http://time.com/3682311/mindfulness-math on September 14, 2015.

O'Neill, A. (2002). *The recess queen*. New York: Scholastic.

Our Documents. (n.d.). *Transcript of President Andrew Jackson's message to Congress 'On Indian Removal' (1830)*. Accessed at www.ourdocuments.gov/doc.php?flash=true&doc=25&page=transcript on September 14, 2015.

Palacio, R. J. (2012). *Wonder*. New York: Knopf.

Partnership for Assessment of Readiness for College and Careers. (2012, August). *PARCC model content frameworks: English language arts/literacy, grades 3–11* (Version 2.0). Accessed at www.parcconline.org/files/131/MCF%20K2%20Published%20Frameworks/258/PARCCMCFELALiteracyAugust2012_FINAL.pdf on September 14, 2015.

Peacock, L. (2007). *Crossing the Delaware: A history in many voices*. New York: Alladin.

Pearson, P. D. (2013). Research foundations of the Common Core State Standards in English language arts. In S. B. Neuman & L. B. Gambrell (Eds.), *Quality reading instruction in the age of Common Core standards* (pp. 237–262). Newark, DE: International Reading Association.

Pearson, P. D., & Gallagher, M. C. (1983). The instruction of reading comprehension. *Contemporary Educational Psychology, 8*(3), 317–344.

Pearson, P. D., & Hiebert, E. H. (2014). The state of the field: Qualitative analyses of text complexity. *Elementary School Journal, 115*(2), 161–183.

Pennsylvania Department of Education. (n.d.). *Depth of Knowledge (DOK) levels*. Accessed at https://static.pdesas.org/content/documents/M1-Slide_19_DOK_Wheel_Slide.pdf on September 15, 2015.

Pinkney, A. D. (2006). *Duke Ellington: The piano prince and his orchestra*. New York: Hyperion Books.

Pinkney, J. (2000). *Aesop's fables*. New York: SeaStar Books.

Pressley, M. (2006). *Reading instruction that works: The case for balanced teaching* (3rd ed.). New York: Guilford Press.

Quindlen, A. (1988). Melting pot. In *Living out loud* (pp. 255–258). New York: Ballantine Books.

Rey, H. A. (1954). *Find the constellations.* Boston: Houghton Mifflin.

Richards, I. A. (1929). *Practical criticism: A study of literary judgment.* London: Kegan Paul, Trench, Trubner.

Rosen, L. (2013, April 24). *How much technology should you let your children use?* Accessed at www.huffingtonpost.com/dr-larry-rosen/how-much-technology-shoul_b_3142227.html on September 14, 2015.

Rosenblatt, L. M. (1978). *The reader, the text, the poem: The transactional theory of the literary work.* Carbondale: Southern Illinois University Press.

Ryan, P. M. (2000). *Esperanza rising.* New York: Scholastic.

Rylant, C. (1987–2007). *Henry and Mudge* series (Books 1–29). New York: Simon & Schuster.

Salisbury, G. (1994). *Under the blood-red sun.* New York: Dell Laurel-Leaf.

Sandler, M. W. (2013). *Imprisoned: The betrayal of Japanese Americans during World War II.* New York: Walker Books for Young Readers.

Say, A. (2000). *The sign painter.* Boston: Houghton Mifflin.

Searle, J. R. (1995). *The construction of social reality.* New York: Free Press.

Shakespeare, W. (1960). *The tragedy of Macbeth.* New Haven, CT: Yale University Press.

Shanahan, T. (2013, January 18). *Q & A on all things Common Core.* Accessed at www.shanahanonliteracy.com/2013/01/recently-i-participated-in-webinar-for.html on September 14, 2015.

Shanahan, T. (2014a, November 10). *Prior knowledge: Can we really level the playing field?* Accessed at www.shanahanonliteracy.com/2014/11/prior-knowledge-can-we-really-level.html on June 10, 2015.

Shanahan, T. (2014b, November 17). *Prior knowledge part 2.* Accessed at www.shanahanonliteracy.com/search/label/Reading%20comprehension?updated-max=2014–12–29T14:15:00–08:00&max-results=20&start=5&by-date=false on September 14, 2015.

Shanahan, T. (2014c). Should we teach students at their reading levels? Consider the research when personalizing your lesson plans. *Reading Today*, *32*(2), 14–15.

Shepard, L. A. (2008). Formative assessment: Caveat emptor. In C. A. Dwyer (Ed.), *The future of assessment: Shaping teaching and learning* (pp. 279–303). Mahwah, NJ: Erlbaum.

Short, K. G., & Harste, J. C. (1996). *Creating classrooms for authors and inquirers* (2nd ed.). Portsmouth, NH: Heinemann.

Sisson, D., & Sisson, B. (2014). The renaissance of close reading: A review of historical and contemporary perspectives. *California Reader*, *47*(4), 8–16.

Snow, C. E. (2002, January). *Reading for understanding: Toward an R&D program in reading comprehension*. Santa Monica, CA: RAND. Accessed at www.rand.org /pubs/monograph_reports/MR1465.html on September 14, 2015.

Snow, C. E. (2013, June 6). *Cold versus warm close reading: Stamina and the accumulation of misdirection*. Accessed at www.reading.org/reading-today/research /post/lrp/2013/06/06/cold-versus-warm-close-reading-stamina-and-the -accumulation-of-misdirection#sthash.0qu4fuzH.dpuf on January 16, 2015.

Snow, C. E., Burns, M. S., & Griffin, P. (Eds.). (1998). *Preventing reading difficulties in young children*. Washington, DC: National Academy Press.

Spilsbury, L., & Spilsbury, R. (2010). *Howling hurricanes*. Chicago: Heinemann Library.

Stenner, A. J., Koons, H., & Swartz, C. W. (2010). *Text complexity and developing expertise in reading*. Durham, NC: MetaMetrics.

Swain, G. (2012). Margaret Batchelder, immigrant inspector. In *Hope and tears: Ellis Island voices* (pp. 46–47). Honesdale, PA: Calkins Creek.

Teaching Tolerance. (2015, March). *Appendix D: A tool for selecting diverse texts*. Montgomery, AL: Southern Poverty Law Center. Accessed at www.tolerance.org /sites/default/files/general/Appendix%20D%20Text%20Selection%20Tool%20 2015_v3_final.pdf on September 14, 2015.

Tharp, R. (1993). Institutional and social context of educational reform. In E. A. Forman, N. Minick, & C. A. Stone (Eds.), *Contexts for learning: Sociocultural dynamics in children's development* (pp. 269–282). New York: Oxford University Press.

Thomson, S. L. (2010). *Where do polar bears live?* New York: HarperCollins.

Thurber, J. (1942). The secret life of Walter Mitty. In *My work—and welcome to it* (pp. 72–81). New York: Harcourt Brace.

Thurber, J. (1950). *The 13 clocks*. New York: Simon & Schuster.

Twain, M. (1994). *The adventures of Huckleberry Finn*. New York: Morrow. (Original work published 1884)

Valencia, S. W. (n.d.). *Going beyond text complexity: Considering text-task scenarios in understanding comprehension* [Slideshow]. Accessed at www.textproject.org/assets /library/powerpoints/Valencia-Going-Beyond-Text-Complexity.pdf on March 1, 2015.

Valencia, S. W., Wixson, K. K., & Pearson, P. D. (2014). Putting text complexity in context: Refocusing on comprehension of complex text. *Elementary School Journal, 115*(2), 270–289.

Vancouver Aquarium. (2012, September 27). *Sunflower star has weird way of eating* [Video file]. Accessed at www.youtube.com/watch?v=l6dnmLDu6Eg on September 14, 2015.

Vescio, V., Ross, D., & Adams, A. (2008). A review of research on the impact of professional learning communities on teaching practice and student learning. *Teaching and Teacher Education, 24*(1), 80–91.

Vygotsky, L. S. (1978). *Mind in society: The development of higher psychological processes*. Cambridge, MA: Harvard University Press.

Weather Wiz Kids. (n.d.). *Hurricanes*. Accessed at www.weatherwizkids.com/weather -hurricane.htm on May 20, 2015.

Webb, N. (1997). *Criteria for alignment of expectations and assessments on mathematics and science education* (Research Monograph No. 6). Washington, DC: Council of Chief State School Officers.

Webb, N. L. (1999). *Alignment of science and mathematics standards and assessments in four states* (Research Monograph No. 18). Washington, DC: Council of Chief State School Officers.

Webb, N. L., Alt, M., Ely, R., Cormier, M., & Vesperman, B. (2005). *Web alignment tool*. Madison: Wisconsin Center of Educational Research, University of Wisconsin–Madison. Accessed at https://static.pdesas.org/content/documents /M1-Slide_19_DOK_Wheel_Slide.pdf on November 9, 2015.

Webb, N. L., Alt, M., Ely, R., Cormier, M., & Vesperman, B. (2006). The web alignment tool: Development, refinement, and dissemination. In State Collaboration on Assessment and Student Standards (SCASS), *Aligning assessment to guide the learning of all students: Six reports*. Washington, DC: Council of Chief State School Officers.

Wein, E. (2012). *Code name verity*. New York: Hyperion Books.

Wessling, S. B. (n.d.). *Simplifying text complexity* [Video file]. Accessed at www
.teachingchannel.org/videos/simplifying-text-complexity on January 16, 2015.

Whelan, G. (2000). *Homeless bird*. New York: HarperCollins.

White, E. B. (1952). *Charlotte's web*. New York: Harper.

Williamson, G. L. (2006). *Aligning the journey with a destination: A model for K–16
reading standards—A white paper from The Lexile Framework® for reading*. Durham,
NC: MetaMetrics.

Wixson, K. K., & Valencia, S. W. (2014). CCSS-ELA suggestions and cautions for
addressing text complexity. *Reading Teacher, 67*(6), 430–434.

Wood, D., Bruner, J. S., & Ross, G. (1976). The role of tutoring in problem solving.
Journal of Child Psychology and Psychiatry, 17(2), 89–100.

Woolf, V. (1925). *The common reader*. New York: Harcourt, Brace and Company.

Yang, G. L. (2008). *American born Chinese*. New York: Square Fish.

Yorinks, A. (1986). *Hey, Al*. New York: Farrar, Straus and Giroux.

Index

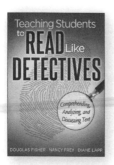

Teaching Students to Read Like Detectives
Douglas Fisher, Nancy Frey, and Diane Lapp
Prompt students to become the sophisticated readers, writers, and thinkers they need to be to achieve higher learning. Explore the important relationship between text, learner, and learning, and gain an array of methods to establish critical literacy in a discussion-based and reflective classroom.
BKF499

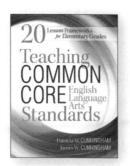

Teaching Common Core English Language Arts Standards
Patricia M. Cunningham and James W. Cunningham
Explore 20 lesson frameworks to help teach the Common Core State Standards for English language arts. Discover targeted lessons to help students master critical skills, including how to organize ideas from informational texts, identify similarities and differences, and write with grade-appropriate language.
BKF617

Embedded Formative Assessment
Dylan Wiliam
Emphasizing the instructional side of formative assessment, this book explores in depth the use of classroom questioning, learning intentions and success criteria, feedback, collaborative and cooperative learning, and self-regulated learning to engineer effective learning environments for students.
BKF418

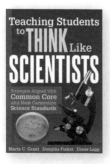

Teaching Students to Think Like Scientists
Maria C. Grant, Douglas Fisher, and Diane Lapp
Using these instructional methods and lesson scenarios, teachers of all disciplines will gain the tools needed to offer students a richer, lasting understanding of science, its concepts, and its place in their lives and the global community.
BKF555

Solution Tree | Press
a division of

Solution Tree

Visit SolutionTree.com or call 800.733.6786 to order.

Wait! Your professional development journey doesn't have to end with the last pages of this book.

We realize improving student learning doesn't happen overnight. And your school or district shouldn't be left to puzzle out all the details of this process alone.

No matter where you are on the journey, we're committed to helping you get to the next stage.

Take advantage of everything from **custom workshops** to **keynote presentations** and **interactive web and video conferencing**. We can even help you develop an action plan tailored to fit your specific needs.

Let's get the conversation started.

Call 888.763.9045 today.

SolutionTree.com